M000099900

THE SCHOOL PRINCIPAL'S TOOLBOOK

Building the How-To Path
To Excellence

Jim Burgett

The School Principal's Toolbook: Building the How-To Path to Excellence. Printed in the United States of America. Copyright © 2014 by Education Communication Unlimited. All rights reserved. No part of this book may be used or reproduced in any manner whatsoever without written permission except in the case of brief quotations embodied in critical articles and reviews.

For information, contact ECU at 185 Shevelin Rd.,
Novato, CA 94947 / (800) 563-1454
www.meetingk-12needs.com

First printing,
September, 2014

► Cover Design by Ali Majoka
► Proofreading by Marcia Abramson

ISBN 9780989653022 (Bound)
ISBN 9780989653039 (Digital)

The purpose of this manual is to educate and entertain. The authors and Education Communication Unlimited shall have neither liability nor responsibility to any person or entity with respect to any loss or damage caused, or alleged to be caused, directly or indirectly, by the information contained in this book. *If you do not wish to be bound by the above, you may return the book, with a purchase receipt, to the publisher for a full refund.*

Table of Contents

The School Principal's Toolbook:
Building the How-To Path to Excellence

Chapter 11. Take Care of Yourself Too!—205

Chapter 12. Tools and Thoughts for the Principal—223

Dedication and Acknowledgements

This book is dedicated to all building-level educational leaders, to Miss Patsy Schwarm and to my family.

I have been honored to work with, and learn from, some of the best principals, assistant principals, deans, and other dedicated building leaders, all of whom have given so much of their lives for kids. "Middle management" in education has the difficult task of being placed between expectation-setting district leaders, boards, and community members on one side, and the needs of students, teachers, staff, and parents on the other. It is probably the most difficult position in education, and if done right, maybe the most influential. Good building-level administrators not only meet the expectations of others, they set their own expectations, help others meet them, and then evaluate and educate toward improvement; all done to provide the best educational opportunities for students. I marvel at all of the men and women who I know personally who do this job with excellence. This book is for all of you, to laud the difference you make with others, inspiring them and teaching them. I hope this book will do the same.

Patsy Schwarm is a dear friend I met when I was a wayward young administrator who landed in a new location and school district unfamiliar with bringing in leaders from afar. From day one she became my mentor, my partner, my friend. Along with Dennis Brueggemann, the other member of a leadership trio that was charged with moving the district forward, we became a true team. Dennis would agree with me that Pat was the one with the intuitive skills, a heart for all kids, and the ability to train teachers, motivate principals, and lead leaders. She is, and always will be, one of a kind. Much of what is shared in this book I learned from her example.

The greatest gift we have is family. They have allowed me to be in education all my life—to spend countless hours at school events, behind doors as I write and create, and on the road traveling to share with others.

Special thanks to my wife, my three children, and to my seven grandchildren (with the newest born as this book is being proofread!). I also want to thank my Sunday school class who make me want to keep teaching and who remind me what a privilege it is to be able to passionately share what you believe.

=====

"Success and failure.
We think of them as opposites,
but they're really not. They're companions—
the hero and the sidekick."

Laurence Shames, writer

Author's Biography

Jim Burgett is the coauthor of two best-selling books for administrators: ***What Every Superintendent and Principal Needs to Know*** and ***The Perfect School***, both with Max McGee and Jim Rosborg. He is also the author of ***Teachers Change Lives 24/7*** and ***The Art of School Boarding*** as well as the coauthor, with Brian Schwartz, of ***Finding Middle Ground in K-12 Education: Balancing Best Practices and the Law***.

Jim speaks nationwide. In his work with many administrator and teacher organizations he provides professional development in the form of academies, video seminars, keynote presentations, and workshops. Jim has keynoted at many of the largest educational conferences in the country, as well as at school districts everywhere.

Jim taught in elementary, middle, and high school and served as principal and superintendent at every level. He was twice named administrator of the year by his peers, and has won many prestigious awards for his talents. He serves on boards for a variety of organizations, both educational and civic. After a full career as a working educator, Jim became the lead member of **The Burgett Group** and continues to provide exceptional professional development. See burgettgroup.com.

Throughout his presentations and writings Jim combines traditional leadership with cutting-edge opportunity. He coined the phrase "Zoom Learning" and has presented this topic to school leaders everywhere, touching on the need for leaders to understand how students learn today and to embrace the challenges it presents. He teaches the way he believes, with a passion to help students.

When his audiences evaluate his presentations or writings, these comments appear most frequently: thought-provoking, inspirational, and practical. Jim's mission is simple: ***"To make a difference***."

More testimonials...

Testimonials in addition to those on the covers of the paperback edition:

* ***"The School Principal's Toolbook*** by Jim Burgett is a refreshing combination of tried and true expertise and forward thinking for principals in today's complex and rapidly changing school environments. I found myself wishing this valuable resource had been available to me when I began as a middle school principal: forging connections with the school family, setting priorities and learning strategies for dealing with difficult conversations and situations would have been easier with this seasoned and straightforward guide. Reading Jim's book felt like having a candid conversation with a trusted mentor."

> ***Karen Bronson, Director of Professional Development for the School Administrators Association of New York State (SAANYS)***

----

* *This testimonial begins on the front page of the paperback edition:*

"... While ***Toolbook*** has no footnotes, it is well-researched and evidence based as Jim incorporates all that he has learned—and is still learning—from his 40+ years in education. (It also includes) anecdotes, case studies and ample examples of successes and failures from colleagues willing to share their experiences and learnings.

What I admire most about Jim's efforts is his ability to coach the reader... (T)his book is not just for "newbies." With more than 25 years of superintendent experience under my belt, I too learned much from this read. Jim's practical advice is as inspiring as it is informative, as entertaining as it is intriguing. While I have a pretty good handle on the critical importance of communications and relationships, which he emphasizes, I discovered ways in which I could not only help my 19 principals in Palo Alto but also help myself be a more compassionate, effective leader... (Jim's) chapter on Zoom Learning will be a must-read for my team. Jim clearly understands how emerging technologies have to be part of teaching and learning... (W)hatever time you invest with ***Toolbook*** will pay enormous dividends. While he would be the last to admit it, Jim Burgett may well be the "most interesting man in the world" ... at least in the field of education ... and after reading this book you will be well-equipped to make an enduring difference in your school, district, community and beyond.

> ***Dr. Glen "Max" McGee, Superintendent of Palo Alto (CA) School District and past Illinois State Superintendent of Schools***

Introduction

This book exists for one reason—to help principals do a better job. The term "principal" really includes everyone who is responsible for school building leadership: that includes assistant or associate principals, deans, special education directors, and even head teachers. If you are an administrator in education, you will benefit.

Throughout these pages we call our publication a "toolbook," a word surprisingly unfamiliar to most spell checkers. It means a book of tools, tools to help you, to improve your staff, and to make your school a better place for students.

The first chapter, "Rights and Responsibilities," outlines the fundamental rights of every principal and the inherent responsibilities of that position. The last chapter, "Tools and Thoughts for the Principal," shares a long list of specialized tools for operations, and inspiration. In between, you will find advice and many to-do lists about developing a strong and effective staff; ways to share your thoughts through effective communication skills; steps to becoming a visionary leader, and means of determining the importance of knowing your own priorities and establishing a climate of collaboration and family.

Other chapters focus on building a staff that understands how kids learn today, and then teaching in a way that builds on this exciting opportunity. It is called "Zoom Learning" and it is changing the way school leaders think. "Team Leadership" is a discussion not on team building, but on the distinct responsibility of principals to be team leaders.

In this **School Principal's Toolbook** several administrators who have influenced education across the United States share their expertise in the chapter called "Expert Advice." "Take Care of Yourself Too!" is a chapter that focuses on different

categories of keeping yourself well so that you can do an amazing job changing lives, while remaining happy and healthy. It is
a must chapter for the often stress-ridden principal.

The purpose of this book is to share the expertise of countless administrators and successful leaders through a series of
practical and meaningful tools. It focuses on leadership, passion, and skills that will help the principal change the world.

=====

"Resolve to be tender with the young,
compassionate with the aged,
sympathetic with the striving,
and tolerant with the weak
and the wrong.
Sometime in your life
you will have been all of these."

Bob Goddard, author

Chapter 1

Rights and Responsibilities

Welcome to *The School Principal's Toolbook*. In the chapters that follow we will focus on specific topics and challenges in detail.

Yet a broader look at the position of school leader is a prudent place to begin. Why not a guiding list of "Ten Rights and Responsibilities" culled from the input and questions of literally hundreds of veteran and rookie principals, most asked in my academies or presentations? Questions like,

* What is expected of me when I start a new job, or move to a new district?
* Do I have to do all of this by myself?
* Is this task really my job or can I hand it off to someone else?
* What if I make a mistake in judgment?
* What do I really need to know to get my staff to change?
* Am I really considered a role model for others?

Almost every word in this chapter is designed to answer those questions, and scores more.

But before we start handling the many tools in the chapters to follow, permit me to say something personal. Thank you for being willing to step up and take a leadership role. Thank you for knowing that great dividends are received for hard work, dedication, and passion. And thank you for also knowing that you will never reach your destination in this profession because it is always changing and you will always deal with people who have needs and ideas of their own. But the journey can be—no, it is—amazing.

Now, let's get to those rights and responsibilities.

#1—The Right to Take Your Time

You may feel that once you have moved from the classroom to the office (or from some other role) that the world is expecting you to know everything and have every answer. For years you may have dreamed of taking the wheel of the ship and doing things differently, or being a magical inspiration, or drastically transforming the school climate with your personality, charisma, and leadership. That may happen, but it can't happen immediately.

You may feel the pressure to perform, or lead, or solve issues with great wisdom, but you must know from day one that you have, and always will have, the right to take your time to make decisions, move mountains, and change the world. Trust me. No one expects immediate answers to tough questions or critical issues. Of course, if the building is on fire you don't have time to review the disaster plan. But most issues aren't as immediate as you think, and a a well thought-out plan is better than a bad plan any day.

Ways to Buy Time

So how do you buy time and not seem like a rookie? Here are five simple yet very effective options.

* Ask for time to research the issue, promising a response date.
* Call for a time-out. Decide your options later.
* Simply admit you do not have the answer but you will seek it.
* Redirect the question to someone else.
* Politely ignore the situation.

I'm thinking many principals might readily accept the first option, and would accept option number two as well, but might wonder about the last three.

Ignore the situation? Pass the buck to someone else? Admit your ignorance? Really?

Faith. All five are valid options—and there are many more too. Throughout this book we will share many ways to work through the skills of delegation, research, communication—and ways to buy time. Let's look at a real-life situation that might bring you some clarity and assurance.

The School Principal's Toolbook

Edgar vs. Brusack

Principal Edgar is sitting at his desk in one of those rare situations when he can devote some time to reviewing the new teacher assessment rules and regs. The phone rings and it is the office secretary announcing that he has what seems like an angry parent on the phone. Should she say that he is available? He says, "Sure, put them through."

"Mr. Edgar? My name is John Brusack. I have a daughter in eighth grade. I want to know the school's policy on accepting homework after an excused illness. How are teachers supposed to handle this?"

The question offers Principal Edgar an opportunity to utilize a number of skills—listening, questioning, communicating knowledge, problem solving, and delegation first come to mind. The principal's response?

"Mr. Brusack, I appreciate your call. To be honest I'm not positively sure how the policy on homework after an illness reads or is handled. I want to review it before I respond and that will take a little time. May I ask what has prompted the question?"

Here is his angry reply. "My seventh-grade daughter was home sick for two days. She was not able to do any homework; she had the flu. When she came back her history teacher demanded that she turn in a paper that was due the first day of her illness. It was a big project. She didn't have it done, so he said she wouldn't receive full credit for it. That may be a major hit to her grade. We've had problems with this guy before and enough is enough!"

Mr. Edgar then asks, "What did the teacher say to you when you contacted him about this issue?"

The response was as expected, "Contact *him*? No way! I've had enough with him. I came directly to you, and if you don't fix this I will call the superintendent."

If you were in Mr. Edgar's position what are the issues you must consider? How does this fall under "the right to buy time"?

There are lots of issues. (1) You admitted that you are not sure about the policy. (2) It seems that this is a situation that might be outside the normal parameters since the "homework" was really a project due the first day of the absence, and not an overnight homework assignment. (3) There is a breach in following the chain of command. (4) History of dissatisfaction with the teacher has been reported. (5) You heard those words that that beginning principal (or any principal) never wants to hear, "I will go to the superintendent if you don't do your job (to my satisfaction)!"

How Mr. Edgar handles this situation will be discussed later, and referred to in several chapters. For now, let's focus on the issue of time. The principal doesn't need to resolve this issue with the parent on the phone or right now. He can set up a mutually agreeable time to talk to the parent after he does some homework, collects his thoughts, and outlines his approach. This is his right, but he has to respond appropriately. What do you think he should do, and how should he do it?

#2—The Responsibility to Think
Before You Make Decisions

This responsibility is a perfect fit for #1, the "right" to take your time. If there is one thing I have learned from interviewing and from talking with about a million administrators over what sometimes seems like 100 years, it is this: *think before you act.* I wonder how many situations would have been handled better, how many cold shoulders could have been warmed, how many icy stares could have been replaced with subtle smiles, and how many times people could have walked away with gratitude rather than storming away with anger had more time and thought been put into resolving a problem. How many times would clarity have replaced confusion, or compassion replaced rejection? Stop, think, then act. This must be the mantra of all leaders.

I was once given a list of things to think about before taking action. I have read and used this list many, many times. For years it was in my middle desk drawer for quick review. And over the years I have tweaked and changed it, then I shared it with many other administrators. I'm told it was a huge help. It is a general list of questions you ask yourself *before* embarking on a new, different, or serious problem. When you are a new-bie in the very important role of being a principal, or other school leader, or when you take a new job in a different school (and thus are a newbie to their norms and cultures) it is good to mentally check off the following steps as you plan your action.

Ten Questions to Ask

1. Have I looked at all sides of the issue?
2. Should I seek advice from a higher-up?
3. Should I ask about legal counsel?
4. Is there precedent for this situation?
5. Do I know who is involved?
6. Is this battle worth the fight?
7. Can I resolve this in a different way?
8. Am I comfortable with what I know?
9. Is there a hidden agenda?
10. Is this my issue to resolve?

Let's see how this checklist of questions applies to the Edgar vs. Brusack example.

Have I looked at all sides of the issue?
The answer would be no, and Mr. Edgar needs to jot down who he needs to talk to before responding to Mr. Brusack. All he knows is the name and the grade and that the student is a girl. He needs to find out who the teacher is, talk to the teacher (or if there is a department head involved, the department head, then the teacher), and get the specifics. He also needs to review the handbook and see what policy the parent has read.

Should I seek advice from a higher-up?
In this case the answer is yes, definitely. When anyone threatens to call the superintendent, or notify the board, you need to alert the superintendent first. It might also be helpful because the superintendent may have information about the parent, the parent's history, or other facts you might not be aware of. Such a warning lets the superintendent know you are working on the issue. You should also share, maybe by email, when the

situation is resolved. However, in most cases you need to simply ascertain if you can resolve this without going up the chain or not. Superintendents and boards hire you to do the job and resolve issues. When you do it successfully you often prevent more problems in the future.

Should I ask about legal counsel?

Do you notice that this question is not "should I seek legal counsel?" In most districts the central office has the authority, or grants permission, to talk directly to the lawyer. If you wonder about a legal issue, or have a question about the legality of the situation, you indeed should go up the chain and ask that question. In the case of Edgar vs. Brusack, the answer is probably contained in local policies and would not need legal advice.

Is there precedent for this situation?

This is a very important question. Even though the "rules" may say one thing, they may have been aborted in a previous situation, which can set either a dangerous or a helpful precedent. If Mr. Brusack quotes a parent whose child was granted more time than the policy allows to hand in work, you may need to investigate the specifics of that situation to determine if it is a legitimate point of discussion. In any case, a new administrator should seek some guidance about how a particular situation has been handled in the past. It should be standard practice to seek history on discipline issues to avoid confusing or conflicting responses.

Do I know who is involved?

In many situations a background check on the people involved in the situation is imperative. Often, when you find out the who you find out the why. Seek information from other administrators, teachers, and office staff about people you don't know. Be careful not to give specific information when seeking general backgrounds.

Is this battle worth the fight?

New administrators will think that most battles are worth the fight, and that is a good foundation on which to build. If they come to you for help, you want to help. Often, however, it is a question of delegation rather than solution. Directing Mr. Brusack to the teacher might help resolve the question quickly at the right level. In this case, Mr. Brusack talks about past history with the teacher. That certainly can't be brushed off. Setting up a meeting with the teacher, Mr. Brusack, and yourself might be an alternative. Or, having the teacher call the parent directly to explain the situation, or suggest a possible resolution, might suffice. Sometimes a situation takes more time than it is worth, as when a resolution has been offered, is reasonable, within policy, is fair, and yet has been rejected. You have to make up your mind how far you will go and how many resources you will expend to make all parties happy. This is difficult to assess at times and becomes easier with lots of experience.

Can I resolve this in a different way?
This is my all-time favorite option. I actually had this sentence written on a little strip of paper under the glass on my desktop: I could see it all the time. It says to me, *"Don't do things the predictable way, do them both the right way and the way that leaves things better than you found them."*

Two guidelines apply here that can be used elsewhere often:

1. Do it right, do it better. In the case of Edgar vs. Brusack this statement means to find the right way of resolving the question, then assure that this process is in place and understood by all, and

2. End the issue with Mr. Brusack being a fan rather than an enemy of the teacher and the school. Is that possible? Of course! Probable? That is the goal! How do you do it? You list all the traditional ways of resolving the issue—read the policy, interpret the policy, define the situation as it applies to the policy, make a ruling who was right and why, and then move on to the next fire.

The School Principal's Toolbook

How about a slightly different approach—read and understand the policy, understand the situation and the solution, try to see if the policy makes sense, ask the parties involved what would have worked better, see if there is a sense of agreement with both concerned individuals, see how it fits the "traditional" parameters, and see then if a change in policy or a clarification is needed. Thus, seek a win-win for everyone. Let's assume that the student's assignment was given two months ago and the turn-in date was the day she was out sick. The rules say homework missed gets an extension based on the number of days missed (excused absences), so a two-day absence for illness would give a two-day extension of homework, but not for long-term assignments.

* Could it be possible that the policy does not outline long-term assignments?
* Could the wording of the policy be somewhat confusing?
* Could there be a misunderstanding?
* Could a one-day extension have been granted as a compromise?
* Should the policy be expanded to include "long-term assignments"?

Lots of uncertainties might exist that may open doors to a very positive and productive resolution.

Am I comfortable with what I know?
Call this one intuition-based, or gut reaction. Are you just unsure about the facts and feel somewhat limited in your ability to move forward, or maybe you don't want to say that Mr. Brusack is just another angry parent and the teacher was right? Or maybe you think there might have been some personality issues clouding the whole thing. If you are uncertain, then take the time to be certain. You won't always be right at every step, but you need to feel you did the best you could.

Is there a hidden agenda?
This question is relevant to many situations. Is the teacher trying to make a point? Is Mr. Brusack venting built-up frustra-

tions over the teacher for past issues? Is the issue really the issue? Your homework, your heart, your leadership abilities, your intuitive senses, and your investigation should answer the hidden agenda question, which is both valid and important.

Is this my issue to resolve?

At some point you will be asked a question that is obviously district related. Thus you may send the person to the bookkeeper or athletic director for the best, quickest, and fairest solution. I often said the following when I determined that the issue needed to be answered by someone else: "I'm going to send you to see ___ ___. I think he/she is the best person to answer your question. After you speak with him/her, please let me know if further help is still needed."

For instance, let's say a parent calls and wants to know when cheerleading try-outs are scheduled and what routines the kids will need to perform. A quick and responsible answer would go like this: "Mrs. Brown, I see on the calendar that cheerleading tryouts are on the 23rd at 4:00 p.m. at the middle school gym, but I would like to refer you to Miss Mulroy, our cheerleading sponsor, to both confirm this information and answer your question about routines. Her email address is _____ and her school phone number is _____. If you need any further help please let me know. Thanks for calling."

The list of steps we just discussed can really help any administrator in the process of thinking through the issue before taking action. Skip a step and you may find yourself backtracking or reversing your action.

#3—The Right to Make a Mistake

You will make mistakes—perhaps you already have! From day one until the retirement clock dings goodbye, you will be flawed and mistake-ridden. It's a given. How do I know? You are a human being, simple as that. The key to overriding your mistakes and appearing to be almost flawless can be quantified in three simple actions:

Plan—Think —Learn

"To plan" means to write down, think through, or carefully outline in some format, what you *intend* to do or say. This means every action, every comment, and every response. I can imagine what some of you are thinking, "A parent asks me a question and you want me to open my computer and outline my response before I engage my mouth!" Not really, but I do want you to open your brain, think (step #2), and then mentally "plan" your response. That might mean asking for time before you answer. It might mean you recall a pre-set, already used response based on trial and error that you can pull out immediately, or it might mean you need to answer a question with a question (utilizing administrative pedagogy) while your brain formulates a planned response, or you might simply fall back on the acceptable response, "I don't know but I will find out, *and then I will get back with you.*" To not plan is to not think and then to respond with some degree of danger or foolishness.

If the issue or question allows you more formal planning opportunities, take them and use them gratefully.

"To think" sounds exceptionally obvious and a little degrading, to be honest. The alternative is not to think, and that sounds almost ridiculous. But we all know that the human has a tendency to act before it thinks. It's the nature of the beast. The problem with this, as any administrator quickly finds out, is that the audience is not very forgiving. Who doesn't know a family that "hates the school" because of one situation that happened probably 20 years ago! And what teacher doesn't know another teacher who gets sideways with the administration because of some decision that happened in the past? We can't afford too many mistakes before we are the bad guys. As you will read many times in this book, when a mistake is made damage control is imperative!

I remember once when a teacher confronted me about a comment I made in the teachers workroom about a student's family. The words I said were heard 180 degrees from their intent. When the teacher (bless her soul) had the courage to confront me I can remember my immediate response, "YIKES! I said that? I would be upset with me too if that came out of my mouth!" And then she proceeded to repeat the conversation, half of which she missed, and when we talked about the words, *in context,* she apologized—but *not as much as I did* for not realizing the situation and correcting it at the moment. Had she not brought it up she would have held that grudge for a long, long time. As it turned out, it was a truly positive event. Even when you do think before you act, you have to be cognizant of the audience, the reception, and the response.

"To learn" means what you probably think it means, *to learn from your actions.* If you do something amazingly wonderful, remember what you did, why it was wonderful, and store it in your toolbox of lifetime tricks. If someone tells you that the way you handled something was really helpful, ask the person why. Their answer may completely surprise you. The other side of the coin is to learn from your errors. The best way to learn anything is to ask. When I first started as a principal I did a lot of short and quick surveys. Sometimes they would be as simple as this example:

Please take a minute and review last night's faculty meeting.

* What were the best parts and why?
* What could we have done better and how?
* What would you like to see included at future meetings?
* Thank you. Your comments are important to me.

That's it. I would tell them their name was optional but if they wanted to share additional information personally with me, that would be fine. The purpose was to do a better job.

"To learn" never ends. And remember that we sometimes see what we want to see and assume that if no one is rattling the cage, everything *is* fine.

Finally, when you do make a mistake, here are some simple things to consider:

* Correct it. Fix it. Admit it. Own it.

The School Principal's Toolbook

* Never laugh it off. Be humble about it, and then move on.
* Determine why you made the mistake, then learn from it.

Remember: Trying to hit home runs produces strikeouts, so don't avoid success because you fear making mistakes.

#4—The Responsibility to Discipline

You discipline all the time. In fact any time you direct or correct or change an attitude, or realign a behavior, you are disciplining. Good administrators know how to do this seamlessly and without effort. I know an administrator who had an expectation of receiving a thank you after she disciplined a student, or a teacher, or anyone. And she usually did! She made it seem as if all discipline was a welcomed event.

There are some basics of discipline that must be acknowledged and followed. They are straightforward—and also very important.

Number One: Never Bite Anyone. Look what happened to Mike Tyson! No matter how mad you may get, how irate your entire being may become, or how much you would like to instill pain in your partner, refrain! Never hit, punch, kick, staple, or mutilate the other person. However—isn't life full of "howevers"?—don't wimp out if the situation requires self-defense or when the safety of others may be in question and you can *safely* prevent harm. Restraint in times of conflict and discipline are absolutely essential. It takes skill and training to do this, but it is worth the effort. This leads to another important basic...

Number Two: Don't Lose Your Temper. At first, you might need to excuse yourself and go outside the room, or just count to ten, or gently beat your head against the wall, or eat some chocolate. But when you are back in control, return and finish the conversation. My first level of defense is to buy time before I get angry and respond inappropriately. I ask them to repeat themselves. Lose the direct look, look away (not down), like you are thinking, and inwardly tell yourself that once you lose your temper, it is likely you will lose the battle. A sage once

The School Principal's Toolbook

told me when I was a young teacher, "When you lose control, the other person gains it." I've also learned through instruction and guidance that the right words in response to the wrong words can alter the direction of the discussion. For instance, if someone says something to anger you, and you respond with, "You know, you really make me mad," or "I can't believe you are saying this!" or "I am so upset with you I cannot even respond!" you have given them control over the issue.

Maybe these words would generate a different response: "I am very disappointed that you feel that way." A statement like that is truthful, does not point to what is right or wrong, and might promote a change in direction. Another response might be, "I'm really sorry you are so upset about this. Maybe we should focus on the things we both agree on." In other words, let's find common ground before we disagree. Calming down the other person is a way to keep from getting angry yourself.

Number Three: Don't Swear. Not swearing is simple, but important. When you start swearing, you start losing. Most people in the position of school leadership do not swear in public settings, and there are those who do not swear at all. But some do, and some swear more when they are mad. Don't do it, and don't allow your employees or students or staff to do it. Set the expectations and hold people to them. This might call for a quiet reminder in private or it might call for an immediate review of expectations.

I had a parent call me one night around 11 p.m. The lady was inebriated, as she often was in the afternoon and evening. She wanted to complain about something a teacher had done to one of her kids that day. I honestly don't remember the issue. After she used the F-word for the third time, I politely said to her, "Mrs. Madigan, I am not using that language when talking to you and would ask that you not use it when talking to me. I would hope you would treat me with the same respect I am treating you." The next sentence contained another creative use of the F-word, and I stopped her mid-sentence, and said, "Mrs. Madigan, if you continue to talk to me like this, I will say good-bye and hang up. You can call me back in the morning." Of course she instructed me to do something to myself and I said, "Good night, Mrs. Madigan." I hung up and immediately she called back. I answered and said, "Mrs. Madigan you may call me in the office as early as 7:30 tomorrow morning, good-night." She called again, I did not answer, and she stopped calling, until 9:30 the next morning. She apologized, called me Mr. Goody Two-Shoes, laughed, and then shared her concern. We politely worked it out. I then told her it was easiest to reach me before noon at the office if she had additional concerns and that I would be happy to talk with her. We got along well after that for many years, and we worked out many situations.

Number Four: If You See Blood—Take Action. It's a different world and in most schools, in most states, there are mandatory rules for dealing with blood. Blood-borne pathogen training is for real and you are the leader in making sure it is followed. It is imperative that when you see blood (a fight, an accident, an injury, etc.), you take charge. When you are involved in a disciplinary situation that involves blood, remember the L-word (liability) and act according to school policies and state laws. Most importantly, use common sense. I always believe that it is best to call parents when blood is involved, and, in most cases, call the police if blood results from an altercation.

Number Five: Ask Questions. Here is another list to consider when you are involved in a disciplinary situation. Ask yourself these questions:

* Should I call the superintendent, police, lawyer, or some agency?
* Have I discussed the situation fully enough with the people involved?
* Do I have enough witnesses to know all the facts?
* Have I calmed down enough to make a reasonable decision?
* Am I following our discipline plan or policies?
* Do I know past practice?
* Am I being fair and just?

#5—The Right to Delegate

The School Principal's Toolbook

New administrators sometimes think they have to do it all themselves. Some veteran administrators mistakenly think that they are the only ones who can do some tasks, so they fail to delegate. Delegation is an art more than a science. When done right it can increase both productivity and morale at the same time. Why? Because delegation can spread the ownership and the joy of accomplishment, as well as having more people feel good about their own contributions.

The art of delegation comes in the ability to ask others to do work, to encourage them, to give them the freedom and trust to get the task done, and then to appropriately thank and reward them when the task is completed. Delegation can also come with some negatives. It can turn people against each other, actually reduce productivity, and divide loyalties.

Some people have the talents to delegate, some develop them, and some never get it at all. Let's look at a few common statements about delegation.

1. Leaders who don't delegate burn out or lose effectiveness.

If you never learn to share the workload, it only gets bigger and bigger and once you reach the limits of what you can do, the quality of your work starts to slide. Or at some point you just don't get things done. The human being only has so much capacity, and in school leadership when new mandates, new expectations, and new responsibilities are as common as flies at a picnic, seeking help is almost mandatory.

Sharing the workload and asking others to input their ideas and opinions gives the task a fresh set of eyes, brains, and ideas. It also gives ample opportunities to applaud the work of others who take ownership for the task.

2. "It's easier to do it myself" results in apathy and lost opportunity.

No matter how long you have been in the job, there will always be some jobs you want to do yourself, usually because you fear others can't do them as well as you can. That may be true with certain tasks, or at least with things that need your single fingerprint, but when you analyze your position—as building leader, department chair, director of athletics, or whatever—

you should be training others to be part of the total operation. The more who can do a task, the better the organizational input and the greater the understanding of what the task involves. When you don't delegate you are actually cheating others from being integral to the success of the organization.

I was once told to analyze everything I do and then ask myself if I could be more productive if others did some of my daily tasks for me.

How can this work? For years I opened my own mail, thinking it was not fair to ask my administrative assistant (AA) to do this. There was also some concern about confidentiality. When I moved to a new school my AA said to me almost immediately, "How would you like me to handle your mail?" I said, "How do you do it right now?" She said, "I open most letters and put them in four piles: Immediate, Unsure, Dated, and General." I asked for further explanation and she told me that Immediate includes items from the state, from legal entities, or letters that look like important business. "Those I open and stack by urgency of response," she said. "Unsure includes mail that I do not open because it might be personal, it's from an individual, or it could be confidential. The Dated pile is usually information with a deadline or some sense of importance, but not immediate. General are journals, advertisements, and miscellaneous mail."

She then explained that I could give her the mail that I immediately toss and she could be trained to toss it before I got it. Then she said, "My goal is to take the time it takes to open, sort, and quantify your mail away from you so that your time can be better spent." I was so impressed and so upset to think of the hours and hours I had focused on doing this myself rather than improving the school. She taught me a hard lesson, and she also took pride in making my day more productive.

3. Delegation promotes ownership.
If you throw a job on someone's desk and tell them to have it done before they leave for home that night, you impose stress and possibly undue angst if the person has no idea why this is so important, what it is, or how they are helping. "Stuff these letters and get them to the post office by 5," is not a statement

that promotes ownership. "Robert, I know you are busy, but would you be able to put some task aside this afternoon and help me meet an unexpected deadline? We need to get these notices about a change in the report card reporting system to the parents. It needs to be sent with the grade reports, and all of it needs to be mailed today. If we don't get these letters included, parents will not be able to access the information mentioned in the report cards and we may be inundated with calls. This will really be helpful. We didn't know about the changes until this morning, thus the need to get this done now. I really appreciate your help with this."

As a result of your explanation Robert isn't upset with the last-minute extra work, doesn't blame you for being disorganized, and he understands that his extra effort will eliminate some confusion for others. The next morning, if you start the day by personally thanking him again for being part of the solution of this unexpected problem, you will affirm your appreciation and his importance. Delegation, if done right, can be a win-win proposition.

4. Successful delegation includes good manners and appreciation.

I worked at a place where one office had two administrators that utilized the same pool of employees for general office work. One of the administrators was a very nice person, but somewhat curt with the office personnel. He would give them work, give them a deadline, and expect it done. Not rude, but not polite. The office staff complied with his delegation of duties. They didn't expect a thank you, and they never received one. If they had to stay late to get something done, so be it.

The other administrator, in the same office with the same staff, apparently watched Mr. Rogers as a child. He never demanded, he always asked. He never received anything without a word of appreciation. If someone had to stay late he recognized the sacrifice and would try to accommodate. On special occasions he made sure the staff received flowers or cards or gifts and always added the other administrator's name. I was told that the office staff would do anything for this administrator and often stepped forward when they saw a task that they could do to save time or reduce stress. For the other man they did what they were told, were pleasant, and did not hold any ill feelings. Both of them asked the staff to do equal amounts of work. Both received a fine product in return. One made them feel important, appreciated, and part of the process. The other made them feel like clock-punching workers.

Successful delegation promotes pride, encourages others to be creative, and allows opportunities for recognition and appreciation.

#6—The Right to Have a Life

We will talk about this throughout this book, but it is imperative to understand a few basic principles about school leadership and about having a life of your own. First, let me give you what I consider the basic rules:

* Family comes first.
* When your own kids perform, be a parent.
* Know how to say no.
* Expect your staff to live by the same rules.
* Your staff members have lives too.

Maybe you are single. Maybe you have a spouse. Maybe you have a family, an ex, step-kids, a mother, a mother-in-law, a brother, a best friend, a partner... it doesn't matter what, you have a life away from school. To keep both houses (where you live and where the school lives) balanced and happy, you must work at it. School cannot trump your personal life. When it does, both suffer.

If you have children in school, whether they are playing with blocks or deciphering calculus, you need to be part of their lives. If you have a student playing volleyball at your school, or a school in your system, be in the stands. Take that night off. Wear a button that says "parent" so that others know you are not "on duty." Arrange schedules so that others have the same opportunities.

At one point in my career I was gone about every school night, to meetings, supervising games, concerts, plays, parent nights, you name it. With luck I saw my wife on weekends, and my kids, well, let's not go there. It wasn't good. So I decided I needed one night a week to stay home. Thursdays were the least busy on the average, so I arranged it so I was busy on Thursday nights.

I made sure everything was covered and simply told requesters that I had a conflict when a Thursday event came up. Sometimes I would be asked, "Can you rearrange so that you can be there?" I would say, "I'm sorry, I have a conflict with that night, maybe we can find a different night or I can see if someone can attend in my place." Some would even be bold enough to ask what the conflict was and I would cleverly answer, "You know I really would like to attend, but I just can't." I never said why, and I never felt bad about it, and life went on. Sure, there were some exceptions, but not many. My conflict? We ordered pizza and watched TV. It was our night at home, and it was wonderful. Four or five nights for the school were plenty. I learned to say no. I learned this from Bert Murphy, a wise principal, many years my senior, who took me under his wing and taught me many lessons. This is an important one I'm passing on to you.

If I felt it was fair to take off a night of supervision when my kids were playing or performing, I made the same opportunities available for others. In fact we set up a trade system where we covered for each other in these situations. I wanted my staff to know that I valued their personal lives as much as their professional lives. And as a leader who made a difference, I put my money where my mouth was. In doing so, we became aware of the families and lives we all shared and ours became more than just a school, it became a unit of caring individuals.

In summary, Francis James once said, "Administration should not be a life sentence. You already have a life, so live it!"

#7—The Right to Seek Help

School leadership can be a lonely job. Think of a district with a limited number of administrators, maybe one per building. Think of rural districts where the time given for collaboration and travel may be restricted due to finances or distance. Think of places where the concept of working together may never have been cultivated, or where people are not quick to offer help, or where favoritism or politics take precedence. Possible? Indeed, and sometimes these are just the cold, hard facts. Administrators are often isolated; as often lonely.

Effective school leaders, especially principals, do not allow isolation or separatism in the leadership team. In fact, they work very hard to build open communications, help systems, and a network of educators who not only are available, but understand the need to work cohesively. So the first comment about seeking help is to remember that it is your job to build a system where providing, receiving, and making available help to others is fundamental to the climate.

On the last day you serve in the position of school leader, you probably will still need help completing some task or fulfilling some objective. But during the first days, or years, in any position, help is essential. So unless you are very lucky and are in an environment that embraces teamwork and partnership, you must exercise your right to seek help.

When I talk about needing help, one of the first thoughts is *the need to know history*. You need to know precedent-setting practices (past practices that, in many cases, become actual "law"), history about people so you can build relationships, and community culture so you have an idea of what will fit and what will cause something short of a riot.

So who or what do you call when help is needed? Who do you ask about district practice, or the past history of a teacher who seems to be absent more than the norm (why?), or if there have been exceptions to the rule that "after three tardies you serve a year in jail"? Hopefully you can ask someone on the administrative team, such as the superintendent, a lead teacher, or a person in the middle management squad (assistant, associates, deans, athletic directors, etc.).

But what if you want advice from outside the system, such as a third-party opinion of your assessment of a situation, or of your planned response to an issue?

What would happen if during your first few weeks on the job another person with similar responsibilities, from a neighboring district, called you to offer this exact type of help? What if someone welcomed you to the job and offered to meet you for lunch, or better yet invited you to their building to meet and talk and build a relationship? This very thing happened to me when I moved 300 miles to a new town, new job, and new set of circumstances. I was barely a week in my position when a fellow administrator with a lot more experience on the job called and welcomed me. He then offered to be a helpline. He became a respected friend whom I spoke with many times. I was pleased (but not surprised) to find out he was probably the most respected school administrator in the county. He took the time to establish a helpline for me, a newcomer. So I did the same for others. You should be eager to establish this type of relationship with administrators recommended to you or whom you meet at area meetings. Everybody wins. This type of third-party local networking is invaluable.

Another source of great help is your professional administrative organization. That is their purpose—to assist, direct, and support. Find a link, or field director, or, even better, another member of this association in your area who can directly relate to your needs and assignment.

But the most important helpline of all comes from building a strong relationship within your own administrative team. Never fail to seek help from your supervisor, an assistant superintendent, HR, the superintendent, and certainly your peers who fall horizontal to you on the organizational chart. Being a team member promotes good team development. Seeking help is not a sign of weakness, but a sign of growth and wanting to do your job the best you can.

And finally, remember to seek moral, spiritual, or family help, such as your own spouse or someone in your family in education; your pastor, priest, or spiritual leader, or a dear friend who may not be in education but who is honest with you and will, or can, help you by providing direction, motivation, or honesty.

Sometimes in this difficult job we feel alone and unsure of what we are doing or how we are responding to a situation (or a person). Sometimes all we need is some assurance that we are on track. Sometimes we simply need someone to say "Good job!" But there are times too, especially when we are unsure or uncomfortable with our actions, that we need to be told to calm down, slow down, think before you act, or simply, "find another way." It helps us think before we do act and do what is both right and in the best interest of all parties.

#8—The Responsibility of Knowing
The Expectations of You!

You get hired by a school district for many reasons. Assuming you went through the cycle (investigate, fill out application, interview, interview again, investigate again, negotiate, sign) you need to know exactly why they hired you, and what their hopes and expectations are now that you are on the payroll.

Way too many people go through the process and forget that they need to be proactive, ask questions, investigate the position, the school, the district, the community, and most of all, the expectations.

When you are in the position of being the one reading the applications and conducting the interviews, you create in your mind expectations of a new hire. Maybe you want more enthusiasm; a fresh look at the current staff or curriculum; new concepts of leadership, and/or a warmer, more people-oriented leader. The list of expectations is nearly limitless. What was it that this person demonstrated during their interview? What did you learn from the follow-up calls? What did your intuition or insight detect?

As a principal I think you have the obligation to share your expectations before you offer the contract, and yet this is not universally done. Thus, a new hire may need to ask, "Why are you offering me this contract? What are you hoping we will accomplish together?" There are many ways you can ask the question(s), and it is certainly legitimate to do so.

The new hire might, for example, have worded it this way: "I want my contribution to the district to meet your expectations, so if you would outline those expectations, we could see if we are in concert. For example, what direction and growth do you expect?" I would love having a candidate ask this question and engage in this dialogue.

But let's assume, after a period of time, maybe even a few years, you still are not sure if you and the district are on the same page. Is it appropriate to revisit the topic? Absolutely! Even well into your career it is of great value to have this conversation. Situations change, personnel change, maybe even your supervisor may have changed, thus the expectations may change too. Maybe now you are expected to provide sage advice and be a role model of maturity rather than one who introduces the cutting-edge methodology.

One of the most important expectations of a school administrator is to be evaluated, often and with passion. Evaluations are simply measurements of accomplishments against expectations. If you know the expectations you can work to accomplish them through your actions.

I remember my first year as a new principal. I was the very first principal of the building, replacing a "curriculum supervisor" who served in a quasi-principal role. I was charged with being the educational leader and responsible for all aspects of operation in the building, including the budget. I was also teaching almost full-time and coaching a sport I had scarcely played! I was a good teacher but had no idea if that translated into being a good principal. To stir the pot even more, some of my staff members were a lot older: one was 70, I was 24.

I felt that I needed be evaluated. I *never had* a formal, follow-me-around and see-what-I-do form of evaluation. It was always, "You are doing a wonderful job, Jim." I never asked the "expectation" questions and thus had to assume what I was doing was what "they" expected, whatever that was. How much better I would have been had I asked, and had they agreed, to share the expectations that formed the foundation for the evaluation process.

When it was my turn to interview and then recommend employment to any new hire, I often asked them to come to the last meeting (where the contract was offered) with a list of what they felt were the top three to five expectations *they had* of the position, and we could compare notes. In a way it was a trick question because I always thought that if we both came with completely opposite expectations, we would be able to avoid a bad hire. The reality was that in most cases we had done our homework so well that we knew before the meeting what the probable discussion would be, and it became an af-

The School Principal's Toolbook

firming discussion, that clarified to both sides what each hoped for the future.

Concerning expectations, any school leader will always adjust and review the expectations they set for themselves, for their staff, for the district, and for the kids. Expectations need to be one notch or more above what you think can be accomplished in order to have goals of growth and highest-level achievement. A dynamic leader never settles for the status quo.

#9—The Responsibility to Be a Role Model

Does this sound too Pollyannaish? I don't think it does. In fact I have the old-fashioned (and indeed still relevant) notion that educators should be positive role models. I think that the moment you receive that license or certification to be a teacher, it elevates the expectations of your behavior to a higher level. Why? Well, it is very obvious to me that if we entrust the well-being of our greatest gifts, our children, to educators, they need to be trustworthy and live up to a higher standard.

How is this defined? Higher standards are: higher moral benchmarks, strict ethical behavior, willingness to make sacrifices for others, a focus on the common as well as the individual good, and the ability to be a team member.

When any school administrator does something "wrong" and it hits the newspapers, or the rumor mill, the public is quick to respond. Why? There is that inherent expectation of trust that parents and the public have for those responsible for the safety and education of their kids, or of kids in general. If you break that trust, even if only in their minds, you may be doomed.

The moment you receive that license or certification to be a teacher, it elevates the public expectations of your behavior to a higher level. And when you become a principal, it goes up even higher.

Can we define this expectation? The principals that have discussed this responsibility with me over the years have quickly indicated that they are held to a higher moral benchmark, stricter ethical behavior, and an expectation that they are willing to make sacrifices for others, sometimes above and beyond what may seem reasonable.

Indeed, the school leader is expected to do the right thing for the right reason, and to be able to justify and communicate who you are and what you do. It is not always easy, nor is it always fair, but it is always true. Recently, at a new principals' orientation, a second-year veteran reported to the crowd that he avoids buying beer in town and doesn't eat at taverns because of the "talk" it generates. And if a principal is involved with anything that is truly inappropriate, their job, and reputation, is in jeopardy.

The building administrator will not always be treated with the same degree of forgiveness as others. This is just a fact of the position, and it is your responsibility to understand and appreciate that it is just part of the position.

So as hard as it may be to understand, you are set on a higher platform of public expectation; you become a role model. Do your job well. Show true passion for the safety, welfare, and education of your kids, and you will be greatly admired. It works both ways. You can be truly appreciated when you do your job well, or sullied by public opinion if you don't.

How can you succeed in this business? Remember that what you do is on public display. Monitor your own behavior. Remember too that if you love kids, work hard, and are a kind and thoughtful leader then you will be the role model that everyone wants.

So here it is one last time: love kids, all kids, all the time; do what is right, always and in all ways; know your staff and treat them with respect; always set high expectations of yourself and those you work with and for, and earn respect through the example you set.

#10—The Responsibility to Be Unforgettable

I remember a sixth-grade substitute teacher we had for about two weeks. I honestly don't remember her real name, I only remember what we called her... the wicked witch. She was absolutely horrible in every way. Does the act of throwing things at students (erasers, a cowbell, chalk) convey a mental picture? How about calling a class "the worst bunch of kids I have ever seen!" How about turning the lights off and staring at the kids for minutes on end when she ran out of things to teach? How about never learning our names? I will never forget her. She became "unforgettable."

Almost miraculously, the replacement was a man named Mr. Ruggles. He was the best teacher I ever had—he made me want to be a teacher. He too was "unforgettable."

I bet you have people in your life that fit those same categories: unforgettable, but you wish you could, and unforgettable because they were so good or inspiring. You have both the right and the responsibility to strive to be the latter. To become someone that years in the future a teacher, parent, or student will sit around a table and say that you provided an opportunity, or you expressed faith in them, or you were there to open a door. Maybe they will remember the principal that was always encouraging and recognized accomplishments. Maybe they will remember the principal who wouldn't allow kids to hurt others, or to be hurt. Your name may be tattooed in the brains of many who simply admired you for the example you set, or the smile you shared, or the way you disciplined, but always let it be known that you still had faith in them, or simply the way you showed them that you truly loved being a principal, dean, student adviser, or teacher... and, that in the process, you loved them.

So there they are, **The Top Ten Rights and Responsibilities of School Leaders**. These are the starting blocks that provide support and strength as you begin the challenge of making a difference.

Chapter 2

Setting Priorities

To help you rise to the top of your profession we must start at the bottom. Knowing how to define and set personal and institutional priorities is where highly effective principals must begin.

Personal Priorities and the Rocks

When talking about priorities my mind returns to a lecture given to a group of young executives. They weren't aware of the speaker's topic so they were particularly drawn to the odd items he had scattered about the stage.

In front of him was a table covered by one of those pleated hotel drapes. On the table sat a large wide-mouthed jar. He began by pulling a large tray that held several good-sized rocks toward him. Then he carefully placed all of the rocks inside the glass jar. The rocks were so large that the jar only held four or five. At which point the speaker asked the audience if the jar was full. Most of the listeners nodded a big yes.

He then reached under the table and produced another tray, this one filled with smaller rocks about the size of pea gravel. He carefully poured the gravel into the jar, stopping a few times to shake the jar to allow the pea gravel to fill the gaps. When the jar was brimming with the gravel, he scraped off the excess so that the jar was level across the brim. Again he asked the audience if the jar was full. Most nodded their head in agreement.

On more time he reached under the table and produced another container, this one full of sand. He repeated the same process he had used with the gravel, filling the tiny spaces by adding quite a bit of sand. When the jar was filled to the brim again, he leveled it off. Once more he asked if it was full. Not as many said yes, having been fooled twice already. He commented that not as many were sure the jar was filled, and that was good.

He then reached under the table and lifted up a glass pitcher full of water. He followed the same process again. The crowd was amazed at how much water he was able to add to the jar as he filled it to the very top. He didn't ask any more questions about the capacity of the jar!

Instead, he paused for a moment, then asked, "What does this demonstration mean?"

The answers were all over the place. Some thought the demonstration was scientific, some though it was about filling the voids in your life, some even though it represented the capacity of the brain. All were well-reasoned answers, but I think the audience was very surprised when the speaker said that the jar represented their lives, and the items inside were how you filled, or lived, your life. He said that the rocks were the most important parts, the foundation of what we believe, who we are, and how we process the other, less important "fillers" of our life. He said that it was important to realize that the priorities (the rocks) become firmly entrenched, are hard to move, and sometimes require a complete "do-over" to replace or change. In other words, it was very important to place them firmly, but carefully, in the order of choice. And then think through how you will fill the other spaces in your life.

As school leaders what we believe is manifested in how we behave and what we expect. If in our heart, we truly love kids, it will be a "rock" in our persona that will dictate how we expect others to feel about kids.

If kindness and compassion are "rocks" in our jar they will spill over into how we lead. Our rocks might be family, work ethic, faith, positivity, or any number of priorities.

This toolbook is designed to help all administrators find, know, and nurture the foundation of both their lives and the lives they change.

When I interviewed teachers I asked them to share their priorities in life. I remember being asked this exact question once when I was interviewed. I had given this a lot of thought by that time and the answer came quickly: God, Family, Work, Fun. Those are the "rocks" in my jar. They relate to each other, but each rock has its own priority.

You might think that in an interview at a public school you might not share them in that order. Don't most employers want you to put "Work" on top? But when I explained my rationale, they seemed to understand and accept it. I told them that what I believe, my faith, sets the standards for my life. The Golden Rule, the concepts of servant leadership, my relationship with my church. And that I had to pick a place to work that honored freedom of religion and supported a person's choice. I then told them that my family was obviously my next priority because I was responsible to them and for them. I wanted my children (or grandchildren) to attend the best school possible, to live in a safe and productive community, and to be able to grow and become givers rather than takers. I told them that I could accomplish all those goals through my work, and thus it too was a top priority, especially the work of helping build a positive learning environment with loving and caring teachers and staff members.

Then I told them that the priority of "fun" was like the sand. It was accomplished by blending it into all aspects of my life—church, family, and work. If the other parts of my life weren't fun, or if I couldn't add fun through them, then life was boring and I would be boring too.

Having and knowing your priorities is a first step to being a well-grounded and successful school leader. If you truly believe that family comes first, then a principal or dean or assistant principal who is given some evening or after-school responsibilities will also find the means to be available when their own kids, or grandkids, are performing, playing, or needing an audience. And, a caring, respectful administrator helps employees do the same, to be available for their own kids.

Knowing your priorities is essential to having a satisfying and well-balanced life. A good leader will help others understand that living their priorities is important. But a highly effective leader will do even more, he/she will find ways to insure that fulfilling their priorities is possible too.

The School Principal's Toolbook

Here's a real example of putting this concept to work. A teacher approached the principal and said her daughter was having trouble at college and would need to come home for a while to work some things out. It was obviously a very troubling time for the family. She said she wanted to be up-front with the administrator and tell him that she would not be in school on Friday because she needed to drive Thursday night to bring the daughter home. The principal asked if she was asking for a personal leave day, and the teacher said she had already taken her day and would need to be docked since she was not coming in.

The principal was caught in the "contractual" dilemma. If the teacher lied and called in sick she would get the time off. If she handled the situation honestly, she would have to be docked. Neither option seemed fair or right. She should not be docked for missed time but still the principal needed to follow the contract as best he could.

First, he thanked her for her honesty. Next he asked if there was anything they could do at school to facilitate some help for the daughter. Would the school counselor or the care program that came with the health insurance help? Would it help if he talked with the daughter? He offered about everything he could think of, and then he asked her if she would be willing to trade a day and a half during the summer to help him review the achievement tests when the scores arrived. She thought this question was kind of off topic, but she said she would be happy to. He then said that since he could not pay her to help with this task he would offer her a trade. She could take off early Thursday and have Friday off as well, in exchange. (He knew the drive to the college was a long one and that leaving early would help her avoid some busy traffic.) The teacher began to weep, and said she didn't know how to thank him. "Oh, you will find out when we go through all those test scores!" he responded. She left his office both relieved and in full understanding that her leader was compassionate and able to solve problems.

The story doesn't end there. The principal went to the president of the district's association immediately after school to share his solution with him, so that he would understand that fulfilling the contract was important, but meeting the needs of the individual was equally as important. The president said, "Thank you for doing the best you can in this situation. We appreciate it." Being honest and fair were two of his priorities. Through his examples he helped develop the same attitudes throughout the school.

Do you know your priorities? Do you help your staff develop and live by theirs?

Handling the Baggage

When I tell teachers and administrators that an item not listed in their job description is that of baggage handler, I see lots of narrowed eyes and an uncertain tilt of the head. You can see them asking themselves, "Baggage handler? What does that mean?"

I then remind them that almost every morning I see them enter the school with some sort of baggage in their hands—a backpack for the younger teachers, a briefcase or bag for others. Some even have plastic crates or wheeled suitcases. A few have stacks of papers under their arms. Many also tote or carry their computer or tablet cases. They carry work from home to school, and then back home at night.

"Now I get it," some think. But that's not the baggage I'm talking about.

The most important baggage they must handle has no handles. Beyond their carry-ins and carry-outs to and from the school, their life baggage might take the form of balancing their finances; dealing with an aging parent; or a family member losing their job, or hours of work, or wages. It might be a loved one's addiction, anger, or instability. It may be a wayward child or an unhappy relationship. Some of that baggage may be transitory, some long-term. Whatever, they have to handle it.

The highly effective school leader sees teacher or staff members walking through the school doors in the morning and knows the extra burden they are carrying. If possible, the leader takes note and seeks appropriate ways to help.

But their baggage handling gets worse when they enter the schoolhouse doors. That's because every student walking through those same doors has their own baggage issues—and they have far fewer means or ways to lift its weight.

Students seldom can live their lives by their own priorities. They have fewer tools and too often they are pressed between parents and siblings likewise overburdened. They are limited by their home environment. They may arrive with less than optimal sleep because of arguments between parents or other adults. Maybe a negligent adult was late, didn't show, or was incapable of providing a ride, or failed to pack a lunch or provide clean clothes. Maybe the kid is dealing with personal issues and no one at home listens, or is there to help, or nobody knows or even cares. Maybe the frustration is another class they don't understand, or homework they can't do. I could list 100 possible kinds of "baggage" that the student might be carrying—all needing the "handling" of a caring and effective educator who has been trained and encouraged by a caring and effective principal.

So when teachers walk into school handling their own baggage they often don't have the inclination, attitude, or energy to help detect, then handle, that of the students. It may be no different for you: your baggage can prevent you from helping your teachers.

What's the solution to personal baggage that gets in the way of meeting the needs of others? How can highly effective principals help lighten the baggage of the staff, the students, and themselves?

A sign at the front gate saying "check all baggage at the door and move on..." won't work. Life isn't that simple. We need a leader to step in, an expert to lead the way. The highly effective leader is usually a complex person able to multi-task, see the big picture as well as the details, and communicate with a high degree of clarity.

When leaders are able to walk into the school with a clear mind, or at least a mind that has personal matters under control, they can, and will, see the needs of others more clearly.

The old adage, "When Mamma ain't happy, nobody's happy," certainly applies here. When the head of everything has his/her own head clogged with worries, the effective leader can sometimes falter.

Even principals sometimes need to seek assistance to manage their own baggage, to adjust the issues in their lives. Professional help, sharing ideas with those you report to, seeking help outside of school—there are many ways and many people to turn to. Seeking help is the sign of a strong leader and one that knows the value of positive change.

It is imperative then that two things need to happen for the school principal, or dean, or assistant principal or anyone responsible for the success of a school or its parts, to be highly effective: (1) they must clearly know their priorities and live by them, and (2) they must come to school with a mind uncluttered by outside stress and pressure.

One more thing about baggage: highly effective leaders make sure that their staff, especially those dealing with students, understands the concept of baggage handling and how important it is to look for signs and reasons why kids struggle or display changing behaviors or attitudes. A leader who witnesses an employee or a student who normally is happy and productive all of a sudden become quiet or sad needs to seek the reason for the change. When a good student starts to fall in productivity, when a teacher starts to miss days, when a custodian all of a sudden stops doing the great job they are known for, when a secretary who is usually right on with details begins to miss things, these are the signs that something is personally amiss. Highly effective leaders, in the office or in the classroom, look for others' out-of-sync behaviors and seek solutions.

Highly effective school principals know that when baggage handling is a priority, achievement excels and people are happier.

Administrative Priorities—Be Visible

If I were to list the things that make the biggest difference between an adequate administrator and an excellent one, visibility would be near the top of the list. But it must be positive and meaningful visibility. The principal or administrator that works behind a desk, hides from human contact, and runs the ship from the bridge, seldom to be seen by the sailors, is far less supported or appreciated than the captain who knows the names of the crew members and knows how hard they work... because their captain is with them.

Want to be appreciated? Then appreciate. Want people to work for you? Then work for them. When they see your car in the lot when they get to work and they see you in the halls greeting, meeting, steering, advising, and helping, you become someone to admire and appreciate. Not everyone's job description allows them to do the things that I am suggesting but if you can relate to any of the following, then consider implementing them, if you don't already.

1. Speak to everyone on your staff at least three times a week—more if you can.
2. Walk through classrooms as frequently as possible. Try for every other day. Greet and speak to staff and students but try not to be disruptive.
3. Eat with staff members or students. If this isn't possible, visit them during lunch for a minute or two.
4. Keep a book with a separate page for every employee. Keep it updated with data such as family members, events in their lives, home addresses, and notes from your last visit. This keeps you up-to-the-minute with things you should remember, plus things they will appreciate.
5. When a tragedy happens to employees (the loss of a spouse, a house fire, the death of close relative, an accident, or the like), write it in your book and put it on your calendar one year from the time it happened. Put a card on their desk before school starts on the anniversary that simply states you are thinking about them.

6. Greet visitors personally. Ask the office to buzz you when a new parent arrives or a new citizen comes for a visit. A personal greeting means a lot. Follow it up with a thank-you note.
7. Be at a door at special events to welcome folks, but never "post" yourself at the same door for the same length of time. Why? Because people will expect you to be there and if you aren't they will think you are absent.
8. Send lots of notes, emails, or texts to staff members for a job well done. An example would be to the cook for great lasagna at lunch, or to the coach after a tough loss at a well-played game with good sportsmanship, or to a teacher when you saw kids engaged and learning. Short notes, not evaluations, make a difference.
9. If you see someone who needs correction, do it, but if it requires a discussion, make it personal and private.
10. Congratulate whomever deserves it whenever you can.
11. Carry a digital camera in your pocket and take pictures, then share them.
12. Smile a lot. Be positive.
13. Discipline when needed.
14. Carry a clipboard or something visible like a cell phone, to take notes when people ask you questions or want an answer.
15. Follow up on questions. Provide answers ASAP. Keep a record.
16. Go to see someone rather than sending an email, text, or message.
17. Pick up trash, wipe off marks, be a visible owner and protector of the property.
18. Pat kids on the back; staff too. Shake hands. Be friendly.
19. Have fun. Be fun. Make school fun.
20. Love your job and show everyone how much.

The Slide

This is an art that pays dividends. Learn the art of sliding when you have multiple events to attend to in one evening, or when you don't want to spend the entire night at a single event, or when you might want to check in at a game, go back to the office and work, and check in later.

To slide means you show up at unexpected locations to be seen. You might be there as people arrive or when the game, concert, science night, etc., begins. You walk around, meet and greet, or watch the game or other event on your feet, never sitting. You might be visible at halftime, but sometime during the event, you leave through an exit and head down the hall into oblivion. I can remember many times when we had two or three events going on in different gyms or rooms and I attended each, "sliding" in and out and no one knew the difference. I would never set a pattern because once you do you are missed if your spot is vacant. I also slipped in trips to the office throughout the night to catch up on work, between sliding in and out of events. You get a lot of exposure; you get to see kids play, sing, or compete, and people know you are there. No one really knows where you are, only that you are "there."

The second part of "sliding" is following up with coaches, class sponsors, band directors, FFA teachers, reading specialists, and dozens more with a note or email at the end of the evening. It might include a comment on how much you enjoyed a certain piece at the concert, the way the kids behaved, or whatever you thought was noteworthy. It's also a good way to mention how proud you are of the coach, sponsor, or kids. I would even thank the folks who were on duty supervising or handling concessions. You earn a lot of points with these types of messages. Sometimes I would even share that I was attending multiple activities and wish I could have seen the entire event. I always tried to be transparent and honest.

Administrative Priorities—Do Right

Desmond Tutu once said, "Do your little bit of good where you are; it's those little bits of good put together that overwhelm the world."

Thomas Huxley also said, "It is not who is right, but what is right that is important."

Goodness and honesty, and doing what is right, should be your mantra. A bit corny but it is absolutely the difference between the administrator who is remembered fondly and the one who people wish they could forget.

There will be times—dozens, no, hundreds of them—when you encounter an enemy, at least from their perspective. You need to move them over to your side: the side of what is right for kids, and thus right for them. One of my favorite quotes is from Abraham Lincoln when he said, "The best way to destroy an enemy is to make him your friend." How do we do this? Another quote, and I don't remember who said it, says, "When we put ourselves in the other person's place, we're less likely to want to put him *in his place.*"

That might be the key. Try to "be" the other person. Consider their anger, their disgust, and their confusion. Walk a few steps in their shoes and look at the situation from their perspective. Try to see what you might do to change it. Try calming them down by saying, "I can understand your frustration. You want what's best for your child. Let's see if we can sort this out."

You try to recognize their frustration without agreeing with their viewpoint. Then you state that you both want what is right. The next step is to sort it out, piece by piece, always doing more listening, encouraging them to "share completely" before you begin to unravel the issues. Again, this type of dialogue is more of an art than a science. Sometimes agreeing to talk it through, without raising your anger level or expressing your own frustrations in the process, keeps the ship afloat and starts the corrective action.

When she received the Nobel Peace Prize, Mother Teresa said, "What can you do to promote world peace? Go home and love your family." Seems so simple, and yet that is the bottom line with our jobs. We need to love our kids, love our staff, love our school family, and work toward doing what is best for everyone. Do what is right, and if you aren't sure what that is, talk about it. Recognize that parents give you their prize possessions, their kids, and they want them loved by you and the school as much as they love them. (For the rare parent who doesn't seem to love their kids at all, *we need to do it even more.*)

There is another word of advice, this time from the Dalai Lama. He said, "If you want others to be happy, practice compassion; if *you* want to be happy, practice compassion." Ours is a job of uncertainties, of human differences, of various levels of ability and accomplishment. What pleases one person might anger another. For those kids that come from a family of well-adjusted and loving parents, there will be others who come from dysfunctional alcoholics. For those kids raised through praise, there will be others raised through abuse. One kid can be late for school because he doesn't care; another because her mother never came home and no one could bring her. Do they both get the same tardy? Do you treat the extremes the same way? You may praise a child for earning a C, for exceeding expectations, and discipline another for earning the same grade for not meeting expectations. Being a principal or school leader means making decisions that are right, but even right can be gray. Compassion, understanding, fairness, diplomacy, kindness, and understanding—those are the qualities that help you decide what is right.

Try to be like Tom and Huck who attended their own funeral and cried because they hadn't known how others felt about them. When you lead by doing what is best, doing what is right, being good, and sharing compassion, people will *remember you* for the difference you made.

Institutional Priorities—Be Passionate

Thea Alexander, the author, once said, "I realized that there are two paths you can take in life. One is seeing life as a series of problems, fears, and failures. The other is seeing life as experiences, opportunities, and adventures. It is exactly the same life, but it's the perspective that is different. You can either walk Path A or Path B. The choice is always yours." The choice is not always easy because sometimes our humanness prevails and our energy is siphoned away. We feel discouraged and, at times, think that the war can't be won. When that happens you need to step back and remind yourself why you are there. Why you picked this profession. That the kids make all the difference, not the politics, not the mandates you don't agree with, not the financial woes, but the future of the kids. You need to rekindle a *passion* inside of you that reflects who you are and why you chose this way of life. It is that passion that will carry you forward and deliver you a successful, life-changing career. No one can tell you how to be passionate, it comes from within the depths of your being. However, you can be reminded, and redirected by thinking of the accomplishments, the stories of success, the votes of confidence, and the satisfaction you get when that fire burns and you are energized to go the extra mile for the right reason.

To be passionate means to care. To care means to find a way to make things work. To care means to understand your students and your staff and everyone your job affects.

Passion also means "a strong feeling of enthusiasm or excitement for something or about doing something." Strong feelings. That means believing in something and doing something about it. The poet Nikki Giovanni once said, "Nothing is easy to the unwilling." Thus, for the passionate or willing educator, it is easy to stand up for what you believe.

Passion works best when mixed with patience and tact. The scholar George Horne put it this way, "Patience strengthens the spirit, sweetens the temper, stifles anger, extinguishes envy, subdues pride, bridles the tongue, restrains the hand, and tramples upon temptations." Passion with patience is powerful.

Passion gives you strength and fortitude, but not the right to have a bully pulpit or take advantage of your position. Harriet Woods wrote, "You can stand tall without standing on someone. You can be a victor without having victims."

Passion can be the fuel to see a vision from start to finish. It can be the energy to move a school from old to bold. It can be the difference between *accepting* a weak staff or limp district leadership and *transforming both* to excellence.

Steve Jobs commented: "The only way to do great work is to love what you do. If you haven't found it yet, keep looking. Don't settle. As with all matters of the heart, you'll know when you find it." Passion in the workplace comes from loving what you do. When you love your job, you will be passionate about it. And if you don't love your job, you need to ask why—and fix it. If you can't fix it, then leave. Our kids deserve the passion.

Institutional Priorities—Be a Salesperson

A salesperson? Isn't it enough that I have to improve achievement scores, monitor behavior, evaluate and train teachers, and work with cooks, bus drivers, janitors, secretaries, parents, support staff, budgets, curriculum, the superintendent, the press, cheerleading, sports, payrolls, and at least 1,456 other things on a daily basis? And now you say one priority in my life should include "being a salesperson?" Really?

Really, indeed. The need has never been greater! At a time of falling public support of education, federal mandates about teaching and achievement, waning financial support from government, and constant challenges from the judicial system—education needs all the salesmanship it can muster. It's called *marketing.*

You need to have a formal plan, an informal plan, and a constant mindset. *Marketing education,* especially your school, is a must if goals are to be reached and visions realized. What exactly is marketing? It is the business of promoting or selling. You may need to "sell" your needs and "promote" your benefits. People can't come to the rescue of a drowning person if they don't know someone is in the water in the first place. People can't say, "Good job!" if they have no clue that a good job has happened! You may see and feel some real excellence in your school, but unless it is "marketed" no one else will know! You may be well aware, as are your teachers, that more space is needed for instruction, greater bandwidth is needed for the BYOD program, and a growing number of students need speech therapy services. But the public has no idea what BYOD (Bring Your Own Device) means, or that you are using half of the stage as a classroom because you are out of space, or that the student/teacher ratio for kids in speech therapy has tripled in the last five years. How can they respond to a need they don't know exists? You need to "market" the need just as you need to "market" how well their tax dollars are working. When kids are achieving at the 95th percentile in mathematics for all grades, that needs as much press as any need you are experiencing. At the same time, the press will recognize and validate the hard work of your staff, the vision of the board, and the leadership of the administration as much as the talents of the students.

Marketing needs and achievements should be on the top of your daily to-do list. Alas, too frequently this priority is kicked to the back burner by items considered more imperative or immediate. And many times they are kicked off the stove altogether!

How does marketing work? What if you were trying to get a campaign started to move the high school start time from 8:30 a.m. to 7:30 a.m.? You know that when high school students start school later, research points to improved achievement, reduced discipline problems, and better overall health for the kids. And then there is the statistic from the University of Minnesota Center for Applied Research and Educational Improvement that in one district car crashes with teen drivers were reduced 70% after school was moved to a later start time. *Sharing what you know is marketing.*

Or when a principal shares the statistic that for the first time in U.S. history, the graduation rate has passed 80% nationwide, increasing an average of 1.3% every year since 2006. Facts like this may impress the naysayers while providing support to those who think public schools are still doing a good job. *This is marketing.*

David Turner, former executive director of the Illinois Principals Association, authored a timeless "Practitioner Bulletin" in the *Building Leadership* series in March 2005. The fundamentals of his writing remain as relevant today as they did when it was published. Dr. Turner simply said that the public doesn't understand the federal and state mandates that all schools must follow. In 2005 it was No Child Left Behind, today it is something else, and in a few years it will be yet another mandate. But it is always something, and always confusing and seldom helpful—*unless you make it so.* Dr. Turner said, "School performance is a complex issue and your challenge as an administrator is to explain it clearly, concisely, and constantly." I love the three C's he explains so well in his writing. They are

The School Principal's Toolbook

the foundations of good marketing: Tell your story Clearly. Tell it Concisely. Tell it Constantly.

When do you start a public campaign for a bond issue, tax rate, building program, or shift in school funding? A good administrator with a solid marketing plan never has to start the campaign because it is ongoing.

Do you want to share your successes and needs with the general public? Have a meet/greet/eat session each month with various publics. Invite parents or grandparents, real estate agents, bankers, business owners, or city/police/fire officials in for a one-hour lunch with a tour. Share with them the things that are working well in your building, what you are very proud of, and your needs. A dozen folks will go back into the community and share your message firsthand. (Be sure you coordinate with the superintendent to always be on the same page.) *This is marketing.*

Offer a building tour on game nights. Maybe a chili supper/tour package followed by free admission to the game. Open your building up for walking in the mornings or after school, establishing certain parameters, but allowing the community a hall-walking health program to get them there. Include a guide they can use as they walk around the school and learn about various departments, and more... *This is marketing.*

Use your signboards to give instant marketing messages. Change them frequently:

"ENROLLMENT HITS A NEW HIGH"

"BYOD PROGRAM INTRODUCED"

"NEW BUSES USE 30% LESS FUEL"

"OUR BUSES TRAVEL 216 MILES EVERY DAY"

"4TH GRADE ENGLISH SCORES HIGHEST IN THE COUNTY"

"LUNCH TOUR IN SEPT FOR GRANDPARENTS—CALL FOR DETAILS"

"HOW DO YOU SPELL BYOD? CHECK OUR WEBSITE!"

A message board is a great way to "see" the school or list the needs. *This is marketing.*

Branding

Another form of marketing is branding your product. Xerox and Kleenex are great examples. They shifted the product name from what it is to their logo. "Xerox this for me," is the same as "Make a copy of this for me." "Grab me a tissue," is the same as "Grab me a Kleenex." These are branding examples par excellence. Can you "brand" your school?

"The Terrific Terrapins" is one way to *brand* the Elizabeth Terrapins as a terrific place with terrific kids. Constant discussion of why they are terrific helps to deepen the brand. Here is an excerpt from a newspaper article that helps implant the brand: "Kids from the Elizabeth Public Schools volunteered to help clean up the streets before the annual community parade. The mascot for the school is the Terrapin, and the kids are known as the *Terrific Terrapins*. You can see why as they spent three hours in the heat last Saturday volunteering their time to make our village shine." Or this...

"Yesterday the State Report Card for all public schools was released. Those *Terrific Terrapins* were excited to learn that scores in science were higher than ever before, across all grade levels! They have shared, on the school website, some of the details about the new curriculum and how the use of technology helped in the success. It is a very interesting article that clearly outlines some of the 'Terrific' things going on in our school district!" *Branding is marketing.*

The best salesperson in the district is the one with a passion to make a difference. Is that you? It should be.

Institutional Priorities: Know the Mandatory Skills

What are mandatory skills? They are national, state, and local requirements that you are expected to know and expected to share, and expected to expect from others. These skills include leading school improvement through mandated school improvement plans. Understanding, leading, and clarifying mandated legal requirements. These might include such things as blood-borne pathogen review, discrimination regulations, student privacy issues, search and seizure policies, interview restrictions, dealing with divorced parents or custodial agreements, contractual restrictions, board policies, school safety programs and drills, teacher evaluation plans, and probably a few hundred more. Okay, a few dozen more, but it seems like a few hundred.

How can you be an expert in all of these mandatory skills? You can't be, but you can be proficient and you can seek information before you provide help, as we discuss so many times in this book. Mostly, know what you are saying before you say it.

(If you are seeking more information in this realm, I recently coauthored a book with the deputy executive director of the Illinois Association of Principals, Brian Schwartz, called *Finding Middle Ground in K-12 Education*. It focuses on mandated skills, especially as they relate to school law.)

As accountability increases in public schools across America, and as evaluations move from the stoic performance-evaluation model, where teachers agree to be evaluated during a lesson of their selection and at a time predetermined, to the more relevant national models based on both observation and accomplishment, the building administrator needs to be an accomplished evaluator and mentor for teachers. Also, as tenure vanishes and teachers retain their professional status based on performance and achievement, the need for experts in the mandatory skills of observation, goal setting, and measurement is greatly increased. This is an exciting time to build a staff of excellence that meets the expectations of highly effective, passionate, and exceptional school leaders.

Institutional Priority: Build Character

One primary responsibility of the school leader is to create character. It is also your responsibility to encourage your team to be individualized experts in creating excellence. Your encouragement, resources, expectations, and motivation can pave the way to a school full of educational leaders making a difference in every classroom and in every aspect of the institution. You set the tone. It should be a daily priority to build a school full of unique people that work well together, have similar goals, and have the freedom to express their own passion for providing the best for kids. Character education is a must for all schools at every grade. A character education program (and there are many such programs across the United States) is usually adopted and then reformatted to fit the local "brand." This is a great way to emphasize that certain qualities of life must be presented, reviewed, and renewed in order to be instrumental for long-term change.

Institutional Priority: Implement the A Theory

Do you know this Chinese proverb? "There is only one pretty child in the world, and every mother has it."

I have a theory that I have named the A Theory. Hundreds of people in hundreds of audiences nationwide have substantiated the premise for this theory. It started one day, years ago, when I was speaking to a group of Aflac employees. These folks are borderline crazy with their enthusiasm for excellence. Their conventions and meetings are not only fun, but score a twelve out of ten for enthusiasm. One day I was talking to them about customer satisfaction. I told them that in my field (education) we have the highest standards for our employees, higher than any other industry anywhere. Usually when I say this I get rolling eyes and even some audible groans. I want that to happen because it forces me to prove the point.

So I grab the microphone and head out into the audience for some give-and-take. Here is a question I pose immediately. "Let's say you need to hire a new employee for the office, or to train as an agent. Let's assume you interview six people and grade them according to their ability or potential. Let's say three of them are average or above average. One is below average, two are unacceptable—they don't meet your baseline requirements. You need to fill two positions. What will you do?"

The obvious answer is to re-interview the three that were initially rated C or B, and hire the best of these three. So far so good. You are willing to hire a C or a B and train them, hoping

The School Principal's Toolbook

they improve. Meaning that having a C or a B on staff is acceptable and growth is the goal.

Once we get through that step, I now change the questioning. I ask for someone who has a child in either kindergarten or first grade. Hands go up. I find a victim, oops, volunteer and begin to ask them some questions. My first question is, "Who knows your first-grade daughter better than anyone?" The answer is usually "I do" if it is a woman, and if it is a man the answer is usually, "My wife does." Sometimes a confident dad will say, "We (her parents) do." Then I ask another question, "If you could select your daughter's teacher next year, and you interviewed all the candidates, which one would you select and why?" About 99% of the time the answer is quick and clear: "I would select the best candidate possible because my child deserves the best." Then I ask the question, "If they only had C or B teachers available would you be satisfied?" The answer is almost always no, I want an A for my child. And this answer doesn't seem to vary between business audiences and school audiences, except in schools where the leadership has not set the highest expectations of their teachers. In those cases I sometimes (though rarely) get the answer "If a C or B is the best available, then that is OK." It almost makes me want to cry.

You see, in no industry does the consumer want or expect the very best employee possible. Even when we seek medical professionals, we realize that the best in the field may not be available so we have to find the best we can, even if they are not rated the best in their field. But parents want the best, the A teacher for their kid, since their kid is the best they have. If the teacher isn't an A, no one wants them. So the expectation from the consumer is as high as the expectation should be from the principal or educational leader. If the teacher is not an A, they shouldn't be acceptable—unless they are on a clear path to become an A. So that should be one of the greatest priorities of the school leader as well as a priority clearly known to every team member. We should never put anything less than an A teacher in the classroom.

The School Principal's Toolbook

And Finally...

It's never too late to demand the highest personal and institutional priorities. Nor is it ever too late for team members to change their focus and reach for the A level of achievement.

I love the way Leigh Mitchell Hodges puts it, "Whether one is 20, 40, or 60; whether one has succeeded, failed, or just muddled along; whether yesterday was full of sun or storm, or one of those dull days with no weather at all, life begins each morning! ... Each morning is the open door to a new world: new vistas, new aims, new tryings."

Setting priorities is a daily task; setting goals is a continuous process, and reaching new levels of success is never-ending. That is the excitement of leadership, as well as the challenge. Along the way, when we momentarily achieve our priorities, when we are moving teachers to becoming A's, when things are in sync, *at that moment, we know we are making a difference.*

"You don't have to be brilliant at everything.
You just have to have the courage
to put yourself in the line of fire."

Emily Mortimer, actress

Chapter 3

The School Family

The image of a school, in the minds of most, is crafted, determined, and honed by the highly effective school leader. The same can be said of the district. It is created and sustained by the highly effective superintendent. Imagine the results when these teams of leaders are in full sync, and everyone in the system buys into their vision and mindset! The results can be, and usually are, amazing.

Fundamental to the success of the system is how well all of the parts fit together. A few years ago I had the privilege of speaking to a medium-sized school district on opening day. A principal had been moved into the role of superintendent and she went out of her way to make some very positive changes. She invited every employee of the district to the opening session—bus drivers, cafeteria workers, paraprofessionals, office staff, support staff, teachers, and all administrators. She even extended an invitation to some of the regular volunteers, substitute teachers, school board members, and to some recent retirees! She asked me to craft my presentation to be valuable for every person there, which was easy to do since it has always been my thinking that everyone who works for a school district is an educator.

Who Are the Educators?

I started the session by asking a simple question, "Which group of talented, specialized educators in the room could we do without?" Then I asked a second question, "Who in the room do you consider to be the educators?" I asked a few people directly, calling on the noncertified people first, and of course they answered, "The teachers." Some identified the psychologist. Some pointed to the superintendent. I simply responded, "Interesting." And then I asked them if I could share two stories, one about Sue, another about Ralph.

The School Principal's Toolbook

Sue was a lady with whom I worked in one capacity or another for about a quarter of a century. When I began my teaching career she was the district receptionist and general secretary in the high school and district office. It was a small district with about 350 pre-K-12 students. I had to work with her for district reports, supplies, and the normal dealings between teachers and the office. She was always pleasant, always professional, always neat and well groomed. The other lady who worked with her, who is now deceased, was the polar opposite. I will call her Rita, since I honestly don't remember her name. I probably blocked it from my memory as soon as she retired. I avoided coming into the office when Rita was on duty.

When something was due and it was near deadline, Sue would say to me, "Jim, don't forget your grade reports. They are due at the end of the day and since you have practice with all those boys you might forget." A smile, a reminder, and the report was on her desk by 3. Now had it been Rita, she wouldn't have reminded me even if she thought about it, but would have told me the next morning, when I probably would have brought it in, that "you didn't remember the deadline." It would do no good to say, "Well, I guess not!" Or to explain that I forgot to go back to the third floor after coaching two teams until 6:30, to pick up the report, which was done and ready. Had I brought it in the next morning to Sue, she would have said, "Thanks, Jim. How did practice go last night?"

Sue and Rita were educators. They taught all of us that being kind and considerate pays dividends. That knowing and recognizing what the staff does builds camaraderie and promotes cooperation, and that looking like you are suffering from terminal constipation, and acting like it, encourages avoidance and even negativity.

One day I happened to be in the office waiting to meet someone. I was sitting in the "waiting chairs" when a high school student came in and asked Sue if he could use the desk phone to call his mom (this was before everyone had a phone in their pocket). She gave him permission and he then proceeded to have an unbelievable conversation. He demanded that his mom bring his gym bag to school before the end of the day. Apparently he forgot something and he needed it. He was sharp toned and rude. He raised his voice and barked one final command, then slammed the receiver down and started to walk out of the office.

Sue got up from her chair and as he left the office she called his name. He came back, politely, and stood there. She quietly asked him if that indeed was his mother he was talking to. He said yes, a bit sheepishly. Now Sue was probably not as old as this boy's mother, and certainly not an abrasive or "tough" person, but for this conversation I think the boy knew that talking back might cost him a limb. "You were talking like that to your mother? Demanding that she bring something that you forgot? And ending the call by hanging up on her?" He hung his head and quietly responded, "Yes, Ma'am."

Now, if the superintendent was in his office he could hear everything that was going on. Certainly I was right there and I witnessed it from a distance of about ten feet. Neither of us got involved because Sue was doing just fine.

Her next statement was very interesting. She said to the young man, "Call her back and tell her you are sorry." He stood there with the weirdest look on his face. I'm sure he was thinking, "Do I have to call her back when the school secretary tells me to?" He probably looked at her carefully and decided that this person means business. And I'm sure he knew that he had earned the correction.

Well, he called her. The conversation went something like this, "Mom, this is John, I'm sorry I got mad at you." He then paused, looked at Sue, and continued, "It was my fault I left my gym bag home." He paused again and then said, "Thanks for coming later with it." He seemed to be done, but then he said, "Yeah, I know. Yeah. I'll be home around six (pause). Yeah, I do too." With that he politely hung up the phone, turned around, and walked out of the office, only to return in a fraction of a second. "Mrs. Eversoll, I'm sorry. Thanks for making me call her."

You know what I learned? That Mrs. Eversoll, Sue, was as good a teacher as anyone in the building. She taught that kid a life lesson. She had the courage and the good sense to seize the moment and make it a learning opportunity.

The School Principal's Toolbook

Then there was Ralph. An experienced bus driver and re-tired farmer. He was a great guy on all accounts. The story I am going to share took place the first year I was named principal, fresh from only a handful of years as classroom teacher. I de-cided the best way to know the kids in my building would be to ride the buses for a few days and see where they lived and learn a little about how it felt to walk in their moccasins. Did I learn a lot!

School had been in session for about a month and I started my journey by riding Ralph's route. He had a windy drive through the rural Midwestern countryside in a beautiful, hilly, lovely part of the country. Down in one of the hollows, in an area of some rather low-income families, we stopped the bus and two kids ran out, hand-in-hand, a second-grade boy I will call Donny, and his kindergarten sister, who was a one-month veteran of school attendance. They laughed and giggled all the way onto the bus. The girl took a seat close to the front and Donny went back toward the middle. Within a few minutes I heard Donny use the F-word. Yes, this second-grader used the F-word, not rudely, not even calling someone by it, but as an adjective. I was sitting right behind Ralph and I was ready to say something but I saw Ralph looking in the rearview mirror *at me* and he gave me a sign not to do anything. He immediate-ly yelled, "Donny!" And I heard Donny yell back, "I know, sorry, Ralph!" We went a few more miles and I heard the word again, then Ralph again, then Donny's reply. It happened three or four times more before we arrived at school. Donny may have used the word as a noun, adjective, and exclamation. I'm not sure because I was still in shock and feeling guilty for not re-sponding, but respectful of Ralph's guidance.

When we arrived at school and the kids were getting off the bus, Ralph stopped Donny and asked him to wait a minute. Donny moved aside and all the kids got off and left. Ralph to-tally ignored me, as did Donny. Ralph reached around and grabbed a Snickers bar that was lying on the shelf next to his seat. It looked like it had melted and hardened several times. It looked pathetic, to be honest. He held it up and Donny imme-diately started talking with the cutest look and the most inno-

The School Principal's Toolbook

cent expression, "I know, Ralph, if I can make it all the way to school without using that word, I get the candy bar! I'm really trying! Maybe tomorrow!" and with that, Ralph hugged the little guy and he happily ran off to class.

Ralph told me that he was working with the teacher and they were really trying to get his vocabulary under control. "He does well during the day, and better at night, but the morning is tough." Ralph asked me if I had ever met Donny's parents. I hadn't. He said when you do you will understand. Both of them can hardly complete a sentence without using the F-word. They are nice folks, hard workers, seem to care, but they have horrible language habits. Telling Donny that the word is bad is confusing since his parents use it all the time, so Ralph is sharing with him that some words used at home aren't nice words to use in public, and he is getting it.

Ralph taught me some very important concepts: (1) it is imperative to know the members of the school family (students, staff, families), (2) before you discipline, know the cause of the problem, and (3) recognize and appreciate everyone who makes an effort to share their expertise.

The next day I brought Ralph two new Snickers bars, one to replace the one he was waving at Donny, the other for Ralph. I also thanked him for his efforts and told him I had talked with Donny's teacher and was up to date on the efforts they were making. And that I hoped to talk to his parents next month at parent-teacher conferences.

Sue and Ralph. Noncertified in terms of a degree, but each holding a master's in common sense and high expectations.

Know the Kids in the Family

The highly effective school leader is a person who sets a high expectation to know all the members of the family. This may seem like quite a stretch to some, even almost impossible, but it can be done and it pays dividends. Huge dividends.

Dr. Al Burr is well known to the profession of school administration, having been honored as one of the top principals in the nation several times. He has authored many articles and for years provided professional development and training across the United States. I had the privilege and pleasure of co-presenting with him many times, and each time I sat in awe of the accomplishments and sage advice of this learned professional. One of the things he taught was very simple yet extremely valuable. *Know the names of all your students.* I believe Al had over 2,000 students in his school. He used to tell us that all he had to do was learn the 500 or so new freshmen each year, meaning that he retained the names of the others. Honestly, I find that amazing since I spend a great deal of time looking for my wallet and car keys and I call my youngest child by his sisters' names, working my way down to his, much to his chagrin.

Al had some methods he used. He would take copies of the student ID photos, put them on index cards, and when he saw someone new he would stop them, call them by their name from the card, and do a mental connection of their name, maybe combining some feature to their name so he would remember it by recognition.

I use these well-known five tricks to remember names:

1. Repeat their name as you talk with the person.
2. Make mental associations (visualize a gym for Jim).
3. Ask them to repeat and pronounce their name.
4. Look at their name in print as you speak it.
5. Don't hesitate to ask if you do forget it.

Eventually you remember names, and if (when) you mess up, remind the students, with a smile, that they have one principal's name to remember and you have 857 student names to remember!

Al used to make it a habit of calling students by their names when he saw them; it was also very impressive when he saw them with their parents at an event or somewhere off campus.

He made no bones about it, he worked at it, but Al would be the first to say, these were "his" kids and he needed to know them.

Know the Adults

It is equally important to know your staff, and to know them well.

When I went to my last district as superintendent I used a trick that I learned somewhere along the way to remember my 250-plus employees. I had a notebook divided by school building, bus drivers, and maintenance. For each group of employees in the book I had one sheet for each person. The sheet had a copy of their school ID photo on top; their full name; the name they were called; their address, phone, and email; a brief work history and/or college history, and what they had done since coming to the district. When I ventured to one of our smaller community schools I would open the book before I went into the building to remind myself of the names of all the employees. Then I would review again the ones I intended to see, or might see in the halls. The names were essential. I also needed to remember if they were a first-year or second-year teacher—or a newly tenured teacher. And I checked my notes from the last visit and added them to my now bulging memory bank. I made notes of recent awards or issues to help me with possible conversations. And if I knew nothing, or this was my first visit, I made sure I contacted another administrator (since I was the superintendent, I called their principal first) to include something positive that I could relate. Such as, "Mr. Grandame tells me you have some of the most interesting and engaging science lessons! I hope to see one some day." A comment like this is helpful to everyone.

I specifically remember going to one school to present a student with the Superintendent's Student of the Week award. I went to this school about once a month, so it was a treat to be there. My notes reminded me that the second-grade teacher had a daughter in college who was recovering from a serious leg injury she'd sustained playing volleyball. The note reflected my last visit to the school when the teacher shared details about the accident and that her daughter missed two weeks of college.

When I came to give the student the award, we had pictures taken, and I talked to the students for about two minutes.

As I was leaving the teacher walked me to the door. It was then I asked her how her daughter's leg was doing. She looked at me and said, "You know, Mr. Burgett, many of my peers at other schools tell me that their superintendent doesn't even know their names, and yet you make us all feel like family." I had an easy response, "We are family."

When I left that building I a made mental note that I had talked to eight employees—a cook, janitor, principal, paraprofessional, and four teachers, and I knew something about each one, in addition to their names. *We were family.* You, as the building leader, can do this even better. You can do it with vendors, visiting professionals, other administrators in the district, central office staff, and all the folks you meet. They are all family. And every principal needs to go even deeper. Not only do you need to know your staff and students, but also the parents. A principal needs to keep records of important events and needs to be the one to send cards and notes, make calls, and be conscious of needs, of recognition, and when a simple handshake, cup of coffee, or an ear to listen is needed.

When an employee has a loss in their family, like a parent or spouse, a very close friend, or, heavens, a child, it is critical at the time to be there, to offer and provide support, and to be as caring as possible. As mentioned before, the exceptional administrator will mark the event on their calendar a year ahead, and when the anniversary of the loss comes, they will have a card, or note, or single flower sitting on the desk when the employee comes to work, with a simple message like "thinking of you today." Those are the things that thoughtful, highly effective people do. They not only help build the family environment, they make it real.

Build Family Pride

Here is one more example that you probably won't find in a textbook, but it certainly helps build an attitude of family. I remember this well because I was the middle school principal at the time. We had an important basketball game that night and the last 20 minutes of the school day we held a pep rally for all the kids. Just before the rally I stopped in the boy's restroom, and as I always did, I gave it a look over on my way out. I noticed some writing in pencil on a wall of one of the toilet stalls. It was some boy's inappropriate joke. There was no way I would discover who the boy was, and it was our school's standard operating procedure to remove any graffiti immediately or fix any damage to anything ASAP.

I was not happy about finding this minor attempt at humor. At the end of the pep rally I wished the team good luck and then I announced how proud I was of our students and how well they continually took care of their school home, but that someone had written a message on one of the walls in the boy's rest-room. I was sorry to see this because visitors would be here later. They would certainly use that restroom and they might think that this was how you respect your home. Then I said, "I wanted to mention this to all of you because I would guess 99% of you take pride in your school and want to share that pride." I wished them well and said I would see them later.

Within seconds of dismissing them I could see a group of boys go into the bathroom, then come out and go into a janitor's closet. They got a sponge and some cleaner and removed the graffiti. They were eager to tell me it was removed and asked if I wanted them to find the guy who did it. I thanked them greatly for cleaning the wall and for their concern, but I was sure the boy heard my disappointment.

The message I made at the rally was not a reprimand, it was appreciation for the majority of the students who truly cared about their school. It was a way to reinforce that this was their "home." It worked. And, later that night, at the game, some of the same boys who cleaned up the wall came up to me and reported, "The writer knows, and it won't happen again."

Include Visitors

Everyone who walks in the school, even if they visit only once, they must feel welcome. Maybe they come to attend an assembly on Veterans Day, deliver a package, or sit in the audience during a concert, game, or play—no matter why they come, these folks need to feel welcome and part of the family. This is an attitude, a feeling, and an environment set by the building leader and the school team. I'm not describing something purely imaginary. The atmosphere is real. The schoolhouse is a home and when you walk in you should feel like you belong. This is the goal and it is accomplished by paying attention to detail and by looking at the reality, not the perception.

Chapter 4

Building the Best Staff Possible

I wish we could include with every copy of this book a large foam hand with an index finger pointing to the sky, like the one Cub fans dream of year after year! You know what I mean, the foam hand that means "Number One." On this particular hand I would print the words, "THE BEST STAFF POSSIBLE!" Granted, it's not as exciting as winning a World Series, but in the long run far more beneficial to the future of the world.

Many times, in many formats, I have asked my audiences to name the number one responsibility of the school principal. The answers are usually excellent but most tend to focus on the kids. Some say, "foster improved academic achievement" or "provide a safe learning environment" or "build student confidence." No one can argue the value of those answers. But there is a way to accomplish all of them—all at once! How? Easy. The *Number One!* job of any building administrator should be *to provide the best staff possible*! Period. There is no second-place responsibility that even comes close.

Many educational authors, and most of us in professional development, know that if anyone wants to create an extraordinary school system, building, department, or program, they need extraordinary people. Not just one or two, but an entire team of qualified people.

Providing the best staff possible is a long-term process, not a simple checklist of actions. It includes the following: hiring the best and then motivating them to excel; having a frequent evaluation system that results in continual improvement; establishing clear and understood expectations of performance; culling from the system those exhibiting weak behaviors, and frequently recognizing the success and hard word of high achievers.

Hiring

Tradition dictates the way many schools hire everyone from administration to support staff. The one main exception is the process used to hire the superintendent.

Hiring the superintendent is usually done by the seven or so public servants on the board of education, some of whom have never been involved in the details of hiring—finding, interviewing, investigating, negotiating, and contracting. Yet they usually do a very good job with the process. How do the do it? In many cases they employ experts to help them. They usually involve members of the community or the staff to help craft the job description. Then they formally write and publish a job notice. Many times an organization will help review the applications and then suggest those they think meet the stated criteria. Some boards have "experts" recommend a slate of candidates and then have the same experts train the board in the proper way to interview, even offering a list of questions. Many hours of discussion, again relying on experts, results in a narrowed field of candidates. The next step is to do "home" checks where the candidates currently work and/or extensive background checks that go much farther than the list of provided references. Finally, they double-check everything when they have one or two finalists selected, so there are no surprises during the final conversations. Hours and hours of work and usually thousands of dollars are invested into this process, all with the intent of finding the very best candidate possible.

To what detail does the school leader handle the hiring process? Tradition includes posting the position, collecting applications (sometimes requiring a standard form to be used), and reviewing the applications to select a group of finalists. At that point things seem to differ. Some will start to research the candidate's information before selecting those who will be interviewed; others will start the interview process and then do some "checking" after talking with the candidate. I prefer the second approach simply because it is fair to ask the candidate if you can call references to start the investigation before you actually do it.

Applications

Reviewing applications is an art. If candidates cannot professionally compose an application, it is reasonable to assume they may not be of the caliber you are looking for, though in some cases what they say may trump the written responses they submitted. If they write the application with a pencil, it speaks loudly: toss the application immediately! But if they simply make an error or two, or they have a single omission, you may see something that is more interesting than the oversight. You can find out more in the interview. Lapses in work records, failure to discuss why they left a position, no references from a past employer, those are concerns, though *sometimes* they tell a story different from your perception. Perhaps the applicant comes came from a bad workplace, a horrendous boss, or some issue that needs to be discussed in person. If really in doubt, some administrators will simply call the applicant and ask why information was left out, what happened during the three-year gap, or for an explanation of other missing information. That might prevent a good candidate being lost because of an incorrect assumption.

I remember this very situation when an experienced teacher had applied for an administrative position. I noticed a total lapse of a few years in her application, as if they didn't exist or they (or she) had fallen off the edge of the world. There was no reason why she left one job, no recommendation from that employer, and no explanation. This of course raised a red flag in an otherwise positive application. I almost eliminated her application from the number of quality candidates, but some sense told me to give her a call. When I did, and when I introduced myself to her, I simply said that I couldn't see if she was growing professionally between this year and that. Could she explain? She said it was a personal issue. She hesitated, probably thinking that still wasn't enough information. She then continued, "My teaching career was going along great but my marriage to my high school boyfriend wasn't. We had a lot of trouble planning our future. I had trouble keeping focused on my job, and I let it slide. I took time off to try to save our marriage, but it didn't work. I also had our first baby, but she was born with problems and passed away two months later. After my divorce was settled I realized that I needed to return to teaching. I loved working with children. I applied again, was accepted, and started over." A compelling story that she probably could not have written on her application. I told her that in the future she needed to put a note stating "family health issues caused an interruption in my work record." This would at least lower the red flags to a more reasonable level.

She made the cut, was interviewed, and eventually was hired. I made the decision to interview her based on the one comment she made during the phone call, that she always loved working with children.

The Interview

Once you have a potential staff member sitting in front of you poised for the inquisition, you need to pull out all the stops and do your best to find out as much as you can about how this person could help you provide the best staff possible. A solid suggestion is that you start the interview by stating your goal, and that during the interview you lace your comments with expectations. It's only fair, from the start, to let them know what you expect, what you are looking for, and what it will take to work in your district and with you. It's also important how you phrase things too. Saying "The person we hire will be the best" works better than "We are looking for someone who can..." Be decisive, informative, and compassionate. Also, be a bit forgiving. Interviews are supposed to make the candidate think, so a bit of discomfort is expected. Interviews are not to be simple conversations. Asking tough questions, looking for honest reactions, encouraging clear dialogue, and seeking a straightforward picture of your wants and their abilities is the purpose of the process. Even the best may get nervous and stumble.

The highly effective leader who is part of the interview, no matter what process is chosen, should include the following steps to assure a productive process.

Do Your Homework Before the Interview

Well before the interview, read the application carefully and make notes about items you want to discuss, such as strengths, possible weaknesses, and unique qualities. Search information about their last schools or employment so you seem well-versed about what they bring to the table. Do the same about the higher education institutes they attended so when you interview them you can ask questions like "I see you coached for two years. Why did you stop?" "You haven't been back for additional graduate credits for a while. Why?" "What were the factors in your selection for the Best Teacher Award?" Ask questions that can lead to family information, personal likes and dislikes, and things they may be reluctant to share unless asked. A good question is "What about our community (or school district) caused you to seek employment here?" This will tell you if they have done any homework before applying. Being well prepared before the interview gives you a huge edge and allows you to go to many places you otherwise might miss.

Plan the Interview Carefully
Keep interviews open-ended so that a time limit doesn't stop a good interchange of information. And never make a decision based on just one interview. After the first interview, the second step needs to be done carefully and with rigor, including calling key and second-level references. What are second-level references? They are the people you ask the initial reference to suggest. This gets one step away from the handpicked people who have already agreed to respond if you contact them. These folks should be primed to give a good reference. You want to hear more, so you dig deeper. I always tell candidates that I will contact their references and may ask other people for their comments as well. If they balk at this idea or say they would like to know who I will be calling before I call them, you may feel the breeze of red flags blowing in the wind.

Sometimes I may even visit the work site myself to make sure I know enough to continue or conclude the process.

In all interviews there needs to be at least two people, maybe three, present. But I feel it's cumbersome, unnecessary, and somewhat uncomfortable having more than three in any interview. Still, during the second and perhaps third interview or visit I may invite others to participate in the process—to gain a variety of opinions. Examples would be department chairs, athletic directors, and teachers or specialists in the area of the vacancy.

The final interview should include the candidate's perspective chain of command: immediate supervisor, someone from the central office, and maybe a horizontal level employee. If a teacher is the person being interviewed, it may be the assistant principal, principal, and assistant superintendent, with the leader being the principal. During this meeting expectations of the position, person, and road to success need to be stated, and expectations from the candidate need to be considered. A complete discussion of the evaluation process as well as salary and benefits need to be shared and fully understood. You might give the candidate the option of signing a contract at that moment, or taking it home to be returned the next day, to make sure they thought this was the right fit.

Training

Once hired, the real work begins for the highly effective school leader. No first-year anything comes without challenges. A new teacher, a new custodian, a new principal, or a new administrative assistant, each is important to the success of the school, and each needs to be nurtured to reach their highest level of involvement. What does the highly effective school leader do to insure this level of achievement? They provide expert mentoring. Here's what worked best for us.

In my last district we used a very effective mentoring program for all new teachers. Before the new teachers began the fall term we conducted a dinner and reception that included the entire administrative team, the board of education, and a veteran mentor for each new employee. The mentor, by the way, was a person hand-selected to match the new hire. The evening was a great event, with some fun and gifts. Every new hire was given an advance of several hundred dollars from their first check, which was weeks away. They were given office supplies, some classic books for first-year teachers, and other appreciated welcome gifts. During the night each person stood up and said a few words about themselves. Much effort was taken to insure that everyone left feeling welcome and happy. For the next year the mentor and new hire would spend a lot of one-on-one time and each month the entire "class" of new hires would attend an after-school lesson, complete with food, that focused on topics such as parent-teacher conferences, evaluation, grading, discipline, and other fundamental issues. One of the sessions featured second- and third-year teachers, who shared some of their first-year experiences. One of the early sessions featured the administrators from each school to briefly share "their story" and talk about some of the wonderful features of the system and their domain.

The mentoring system was primarily put in place to help the building principals as they monitored and guided the new teachers (and other employees), meeting with them frequently, and conducting formal and informal (including walkthrough) evaluations. We encouraged new teachers to shine by the end of their first year, and because we did such an extensive and effective job selecting and training them, we had a very low new-teacher turnover.

It Pays to Invest in This Process
It is far easier to "grow" a good teacher when they come hand-picked from the best of the crop. When the expectations are clear, the vision shared, and the efforts are collaborative, you build a school where kids flourish.

So Far...
The primary responsibility of any highly effective school leader is to provide the best staff possible.

To accomplish this end you need to staff the system with the best, most promising new hires. The entire hiring process needs to be done with great passion and seriousness.

Once a new staff member has been hired, the real work begins: mentoring them and guiding them to fit the system, to exceed the expectations, and to become grade A members of the family.

"Building human capital may not get headlines, like opening a slew of new schools or completely re-designing a district's curriculum, but veterans of urban education reform say it is one of the key behind-the-scenes factors in determining if changes succeed or fail..."

Carl Vogel

After Hiring

After hiring, what's next? That's what this book is mostly about. *Your* leadership determines the success of your building. If you follow the principles outlined in this book—ideas, behaviors, and processes proven by successful leaders—then you will move the ship in the right direction and meet or exceed the goals you set. If you fail to lead, the ship will fail to sail. It may float for a while, or even cruise some on its own power, but it will eventually choke from lack of fuel and sit in the bay, never reaching the intended port. So, after you hire, mentor, and get good employees moving in the right direction, you must continue to lead them. Constant evaluations that are understood, helpful, and based on common sense make a good teacher or employee great. Some will get there without much help, a few will quickly become helpers themselves, and some will stumble and need to be picked up, dusted off, encouraged and then gently pushed. If this process is done well, you will see systematic results quickly.

The principal who "builds" his/her own staff, and the staff that appreciates and respects their leader, will indeed make a difference. Positive growth just doesn't happen, it is a continuous, sometimes difficult process. You will know when it is on or off track, and if all parties own the same set of expectations, have the same level of respect and trust, you will be able to make adjustments when needed.

Building Camelot

There aren't many situations where the principal can say, "I hired every staff member and they are all the best." It happens, and when it does it's magical. But in most cases an administrator comes on the scene with an established staff in place and only gets to hire as the need allows. And, as we all know, many of the inherited staff members are often less than stellar. Sometimes a principal inherits some real "challenges." Let's talk about what to do when that happens, or when a good teacher takes a leave of absence, not from the job, but from excellence.

Every human being who works in a school system is fundamental to the success of that system. No exceptions. So if we are going to talk about turning around existing staff members, or realigning those that are leaning toward ineffectiveness, we need to remember that while we talk a lot about teachers, this process also includes all the noncertified staff, the part-timers, and even those in the ranks of administrative leadership. Am I saying a principal can help realign a superintendent? You bet! When principals expect a higher degree of performance from their employees than the super does, it sometimes sets a corrective example. I have seen this happen; I have actually participated in the process.

Let me be very clear before I move on. I am about to talk about one of the hardest parts of leading a school. I am about to suggest that the best principals will not accept anything less than the level of excellence they visualize and expect. It means that if they visualize a staff that is all A level performers, they must work to achieve it. This means that if some C performers are in the fold, they need to improve. If we have anything lower than a C, we need to be clear that their level of work is not acceptable and will not be tolerated. Yes, tough talk in a profession filled with tenure, professional associations, contracts, and "union" mentality. To build a strong staff means that a principal may have to take what was given and then tweak, alter, improve, change, or produce something that fits the "new" expectations. And, yes, this isn't always possible. Some employees won't bend without breaking. Some won't see or embrace the new objectives. Some simply won't be motivated to improve. Some, to be honest, will need to make way for others. They will need to go and you must be the one pushing them on to bigger and better things—outside your school.

New nationally mandated evaluation models, school improvement plans, district-wide changes, formal or informal remediation, and all the other legal processes take time to complete. Every district or state will present a different set of procedures that must be followed to make sure that the employee is treated fairly and with respect. Some of these procedures take months, some take years. Some are easy to follow and some are tremendously cumbersome. But no matter, the objective must remain clear: having on board people who are willing to work toward the best educational opportunities for kids and the best school system.

Cleaning House

Most states require that the school follow an approved teacher/employee evaluation program. Part of that process includes guidelines (usually long and detailed) about how to remediate and possibly terminate.

Unions and some politicians over the years have crafted some complicated steps for improving or removing teachers. It is sometimes less difficult to remove noncertified staff since they don't seem to have the clout that teacher unions do. This is not a slanted commentary but fact. Certified staff members are often handled in a rather legalistic manner. Noncertified staff generally have fewer barriers to overcome, but enough to make the job challenging. Unfortunately for school administrators, some states handle "contractual" employees, such as bus drivers, kitchen staff, or custodians, differently.

The guidelines that cover hiring, development, and dismissal may be in the hands of a third-party contractor rather than the school. For example, this happens when districts hire companies that provide transportation, food, or cleaning services. It can create a problem when the school is trying to make sure that every employee meets similar standards of excellence. In situations like these the district must ensure that hiring, training, and dismissal practices follow similar guidelines and expectations as used with district-managed employees.

If a principal is going to rely on policy and evaluation systems to hone a staff of excellence, there can be no misunderstanding about the process or the end goals. This means that existing evaluation plans may need to be reviewed in order for building or systematic changes to be made. When I say everyone needs to understand the process I mean from board to employee and everyone in between. *There should be no confusion that the process being used is there for one of two reasons—to improve or remove.*

I know that I have already rattled some cages by saying the R-word—"remove."

Do I really mean to "remove from the payroll"? Indeed I do. That is the secondary purpose of evaluation. If you cannot improve, then remove.

Evaluate Toward Improvement

It doesn't matter which evaluation process or remediation plan a school system uses. Every system can be successful if all participants buy into the goals and understand the desired outcomes. A system that is working toward being the best must understand that *employee improvement* is not a one-stop process, but a long-term commitment to regular and meaningful training.

Let's think about traditional teacher evaluations. New teachers may (or may not) get some limited training in how the evaluation, improvement, and performance process works. Hopefully they do, and hopefully if you are the building leader you are making sure that this very important training happens. But either way, with or without training and understanding, they get evaluated. During the first year of teaching they may be evaluated one, two, three, or four times. In future years the evaluations come less frequently. Teachers aren't stupid. They prepare for the evaluation sessions, often selecting a comfortable lesson, getting a good night's sleep, and then "performing" to the best of their abilities when the evaluator is present. It is similar to the bus driver who sees the supervisor coming with her/his clipboard. They make sure every step on the pre-trip inspection form is carefully completed and then they greet and talk with students in an unusually polite manner. Everyone knows that an evaluation made under these conditions borders on being bogus.

It isn't odd that we have mediocre teachers in the classroom with evaluation after evaluation that boast outstanding, or at least acceptable, scores. They know the system and know how to work it, and the principal doesn't have the ability, or perceived opportunity, to truly evaluate when and where and how often they want. Or do they? I'm not aware of any evaluation system that says a principal (or assigned evaluator) cannot do informal visitations. Or prohibits them from discussing what they see during those visitations. If this is not allowed, then the first thing needed is a revised evaluation process that results in true improvement and not some hocus-pocus procedure designed to protect the weak.

Every evaluation process should be based on these three steps: evaluate, remediate, eliminate. Evaluate the performance on a "real time" basis. Remediate anything that doesn't lean toward excellence (or improvement), and then eliminate the weak performance areas or eliminate the employee from the payroll. Harsh? Maybe. Necessary? Absolutely!

Four Steps Toward Improvement

This four-step process for staff improvement works. It is simple. It makes sense. This is not a process for removal, but a process for growth. Even your A teachers grow under these steps, and it is easy to understand why. Here are the four components in simple English:

1. Clarify the purpose.
2. Communicate the expectations.
3. Set reasonable goals.
4. Evaluate, remediate, terminate.

Clarify the Purpose

Here is a truth about education: a small percentage of negatives are allowed to dominate the large percentage of positives. For example, if one or two kids were late, or laughed, or threw a wad of paper, the whole class may be judged, or punished, or pay the price. We sometimes let the fears or insecurities of a few employees drive the process for the majority. How many teachers really fear evaluations? Only a few, and some of them should. But the majority of teachers want the system to do well, they want good teachers up and down the articulation line, and they want good employees to work with, so why not use these very folks to push for a more sane and productive evaluation system? If we want to turn around weak teachers, we need to employ the help of good ones. We need to have them assist us in clarifying the purpose and use their productive work methods as examples. Use the strong to strengthen the weak.

The first step is simple. Stay positive. Bring a list of accomplishments. Talk about how encouraged you feel about the good things the teacher does (or did). Thank the teacher for serving kids. Focus on moving forward. Then ask the teacher to share their thoughts on what they think their purpose is. Then share yours. The goal is to find the areas you agree on. Focus on the positive first. Then talk about the areas where you might differ and try to get a conversation going about why and how you can reach common ground.

No, this isn't rocket science. This is basic *Communications 101*. And, at times, it's not easy to do. The alternative is to do nothing, complain about the problem, let the discord fester and possibly explode, or hope it will go away. Another alternative is to avoid the issue, count the days until retirement (or the next job), and take a detour off the road of excellence. *Unless you are willing to focus on the problems at hand,* they will remain a roadblock to success.

Sometimes weak staff members *will* go away. I knew a teacher who was a real, certified, registered pain. I think she was born negative. She single-handedly caused the positive momentum of an entire elementary school to come almost to a screeching halt. I was brewing up a plan of attack when she

The School Principal's Toolbook

came in and resigned effective in two weeks. Her husband was transferred. I went to church that night and thanked God. It took only days for the attitude of an entire grade level to go up, and then the rest of the school followed. But you can't count on job transfers, miracles, or even sudden changes of heart.

Problems that affect performance exist everywhere. Problems like the teacher with a bad attitude about the dress code, a janitor who can't stand the guy who comes in for the night shift so he fails to communicate with him, the cook who yells at kids for who knows what, or the bus driver who does a full inspection only when he is being inspected. There's the teacher's aide who shares confidential information about some of the parents of the special needs kids she works with, or the secretary who thinks she makes all the decisions. Every one of these situations needs to be fixed. Every one of these people must understand *the purpose of their job* and the importance of doing it well. Every one of these examples can be a roadblock in the quest for excellence. And every example given is your job to fix.

The Expectations

It is essential that every employee understands the purpose and importance of their role in the system. I was once addressing a group of office employees and I randomly went through the audience asking a handful what they did. One lady said she literally worked in a converted closet and counted money all day. She said she only saw kids on her way to and from her "cell," as she jokingly called her work area. I asked her if she thought her job was important. Her response was, "I guess so, but anyone could do it with a little training." I loved her answer. My response to it was simple and short. I told her that all jobs require training, but if people didn't do their jobs well the system wouldn't work. Counting money correctly is the baseline for the accounting department. Everything that has to do with accounting—budgets, audits, paychecks, invoices, financial records, funding, all of it—is based on correct financial records. It is fundamental to the operations of the district. It all starts in her cell. If she messed up, if she was dishonest, if she put money in the wrong accounts, if she made any error for any reason, she could jeopardize the entire reputation and operation of the district. Before I was done I had the audience thinking that our national economy was in the hands of this woman. I concluded by saying, "You are not only important, you are essential!"

Later, at a break, she came up to me, a bit emotional, and told me that she never felt so important. She even admitted that often at school she felt like the unloved stepsister. She thanked me for using her as an example.

That is what every employee needs to feel. Important, relevant, meaningful, filling a needed purpose. You can't realistically raise expectations if employees don't feel that the service they perform has value. When you multiply zero by anything you get zero. You have to establish a value, and then you can raise it with higher expectations.

If the money lady feels valued and important it will be easier to tell her you have found a new software program that will allow her to handle additional responsibilities and become even more involved with the school's financial program. If she understands her purpose and knows her value, you can adjust the expectations of her job with ease.

Adjusting set expectations can make the good employee better and the weak one stronger. Expectations are the cornerstone to improvement. Higher achievement, better scores on the state exam, a higher percentage of students enrolled in Advanced Placement, more solo and ensemble contest winners, a higher graduation rate, improved kitchen ratings by the health department, fewer bus accidents, whatever the expectations are, setting them is the first and most important step in reaching them. *But expectations have to be understood, owned, and cooperatively established to have value.*

The Goals

Expectations lead to goals. Geisell is a second-year seventh-grade math teacher. The school where she works has met the state standards for seventh-grade math for the past four years, but the percentage of students meeting the standards has fallen slightly during the last two years. The school and math department have agreed that the expectations for achievement in math need to be raised. Just meeting the standards is accepta-ble, but not excellent, so the expectation has been elevated. That's a good first step. Now Geisell and her fellow math teachers have been asked to set some different goals to reach the new level of expectation. Her principal realizes that after only two years of teaching Geisell is still a rookie and may need some help not only in setting the goals but achieving them. So the principal decides to divide the group of six sev-enth-grade math teachers into three teams of two, and pairs Geisell with Mike, a 28-year veteran who is also a National Board Certified teacher. Geisell and Mike don't know each oth-er very well.

Mike would probably have preferred to be paired with James, who has been teaching math for 11 years, at several grade levels, and who coaches basketball with him. But James is teamed with Susan, another veteran who is a master at de-livery and a very successful motivator of kids. James is a good technician, but not an exciting teacher. The principal is not on-ly helping these teachers work on setting appropriate goals to reach the new achievement expectations, but is also using the pairing process to strengthen individual skills. Geisell will learn some of the tools that Nationally Board Certified teach-ers learn in their training. James might learn some teaching techniques that could make his delivery more exciting and more productive. The principal then asked both teams to work together to share what they discovered. Who wins? Everyone. Mike and Susan feel honored to be recognized as talented teachers. Geisell and James will reap the benefits of excellent role models. Meaningful goals will be set. Most important, kids will get better instruction.

Evaluate, Remediate, Terminate

Here we are again, the keys to ensuring a high quality staff. Find an evaluation program that helps define the purpose of each employee and the expectations of the job, as well as measures how well the employee meets the stated goals. If the evaluation indicates that the employee is not meeting the standards of the system, then you need to fix the problem (re-mediate). Fixing the problem may be as minor as a small adjustment in skill level, knowledge, or delivery methods or as large as a full remediation plan as outlined by the policies of the district or legal mandates.

Full-blown remediation is intimidating, scary, and assumed to be the last effort before extinction. It should always be initiated with one goal: to improve the employee to meet stated expectations. It should never be done to terminate the employee. That may be the end result, but it cannot be the reason for remediation. Remediating may not result, or even promote, excellence. It may only ensure "meeting standards" as opposed to exceeding them. Remediation is a necessary step if you want to get to the entrance ramp. It's like a basal reader. You have to master the reader before you pick up a novel. Remediating may take harmful employees and give them the opportunity to become helpful ones. However, you must pass "neutral" before you shift into drive.

This brings up a potential problem with remediation. Some administrators will remediate and bring a weak employee to a level of adequacy, but stop there. They either assume that the employee can't do better or they are happy the complaints have stopped, the work ethic has improved, the kids are at least getting an "average" opportunity, or the safety, cleanliness, or general atmosphere of the school or system is no longer a problem. But who just wants mediocrity? Stopping there accepts the average, the bland. To achieve continual improvement, to build a staff of A employees, remediation can't be your last stop.

Time to Terminate!

Does that mean you move on to "termination"? Yes, but termination has two avenues. You can terminate (vaporize, eliminate, pooferize) the employee. Or you can terminate their negative attitude, mediocre performance, or award-winning dullness. Terminate those behaviors and replace them with exceptional ones. Move the borderline employee not just over the edge of acceptance but into the territory of exceptional performance.

When I use the word "terminate" people get their feathers ruffled (even those who, to my observation, have no feathers).

They think they will be fired. You have to remind them often, sometimes very often, that losing their job isn't the goal, but what you want to terminate is anything less than excellence. In other words, you want to eliminate all the behaviors, teaching styles, and attitudes that prevent the teacher (or staff member) from achieving excellence. I think the key concept is wrapped in the word "all." This isn't a piecemeal project, although it may take many steps and may indeed be accomplished piece by piece, but the goal is the whole *enchilada*, new and improved, and doing great!

Will all staff members jump to get aboard this train? You know the answer to that. However, if you do this right; build ownership; develop trust that you are working for them, not against them, and keep dangling the carrot that they will feel better when they do better, you may have more success than first imagined.

Let's look at a quick scenario. Let's say you have a 15-year veteran high school math teacher (let's call him Jamie) who does a fair job with geometry students, a very good job with advanced algebra, and a terrible job with freshman anything—or with remedial anything. All you get are complaints from parents, students, and even other staff with this teacher when freshman or remedial classes are taught. He is so bad with freshman or remedial kids that you hate to assign him those classes, but scheduling and the number of teachers and students make it necessary to give him two classes in these categories every year. Jamie has been clever enough to manipulate his evaluations to focus on the classes where he does a good job. Let's say that in those classes he is B. He has avoided the classic evaluation process in his freshman or remedial classes—at least before you came. But your informal evaluations and the input from students, parents, and staff have told you that Jamie is way below "excellent" and needs to be remediated.

You do some informal observations and you meet with Jamie to cover the four steps (clarify, communicate, goals, terminate). Now remember, this is in addition to, or outside your formal evaluation system. This is your process, your passion, your drive to provide the best staff possible. And, if you are doing it right, every staff member understands your goals and your process. You don't shortcut or avoid the association/district or state evaluation process, you simply augment it with your expectations as the educational leader. This isn't more work for anyone; it's a clarification and implementation of the administrative leader's passion and drive, and this isn't negotiable.

So you start with a conversation. You ask the clarifying question, "Tell me, Jamie, how are you doing in all your classes? What do you like, what do you struggle with, what would you change?" You get the discussion going without judging or sharing your feelings. If he is honest with you (because he trusts you) he will talk. You will be able to clarify what he is expected to do with every student, in every class, no matter what. And, if you do it right, he will understand and agree. Check off clarification.

Now you talk expectations. You tell him what you expect and what you know. You know he is an outstanding teacher because you have seen it. You know he has the skills and mindset to be one of the best; you have seen it. You know that he loves some of his classes. He has told you so, and you have seen that too. And you know that he falls short in other classes because you have discussed it, you feel it, your informal observations show it, and he has owned up to it when you talked previously (during clarification). He was clear. Now you need to be clear too. You state your expectations for every staff member and your desire to help them reach those expectations. Those expectations include successful teaching of all students in all classes. Once again, if you conduct the conversation in a trustworthy, meaningful manner, with Jamie encouraged to do most of the talking, then set the goal to make him happier as a teacher and thus better as an educator, he will help you outline the expectations.

Goal setting is not as Ivy League as you might think, nor does it require a week of intense professional development. In fact, when you corral two or more professional, college-graduated, licensed educators in the same room, having the same conversation, coming up with goals of improvement, it should be quite easy. You agree on the areas of need and begin to set "manageable chunks" of progress, step by step, leading to the end goal or vision. Did I say vision? Indeed I did, because you have a vision of Jamie being an extraordinary teacher, and that is the vision you want him to own. Setting goals is no more complicated that writing down steps to reach the vision. (1) Identify why freshman algebra causes you to be anxious. (2) List the problems relating to students with remedial math needs. (3) Discuss your understanding, or lack of understanding, of working with kids who don't appreciate or want to excel in math.

Those three steps may be the first action toward changing attitude and behavior. If Jamie agrees to invest some time and discussion on these three questions, you may mutually come up with the next set of "manageable chunks" toward the vision.

Goal setting continues as long as it is progressing and moving toward the stated expectations. The speed and intensity follow the success of the activities.

The last step is "remediation" but as you can see, if the goals are progressive, working, and successful, they become the remediation plan! This is how the system is planned to work. You mutually understand the purpose, you mutually appreciate the expectations, and you mutually set the goals. If these three steps work, you end up remediating the issues, terminating the problems, and reaching the vision.

But what if Jamie isn't cooperative, or doesn't fall in line with the process? Then remediation becomes more formal and you become more determined (or autocratic) in your leadership—and the direction goes from collaboration to direction, more telling than encouraging and promoting. You share that with Jamie.

If remediation doesn't remediate, then you need to terminate. Follow the district plan, do what I did many, many times as principal: have an honest talk with the employee.

There is always the chance that the remediation process is not totally successful and, after all the work and effort, you end up with an average teacher rather than an excellent one. If that is the case you still need to work on "terminating" their average qualities and move them toward excellence. Do you fire the teachers? Not if they are meeting "OK" standards and "passing" evaluations. *But you can raise the bar.* You can set newer and higher expectations. You can say that average isn't good enough.

An honest conversation with a new set of expectations and a new remediation process on the horizon may be all that is needed to get the teacher to jump to another district, find another job, or request another position in the system. It may lead to creative options to accelerate retirement or promote a career change. If done in a positive manner that takes into consideration legal parameters and the best interest of the employee, in most cases you can make a change. It may mean a buyout, a transfer, or help with a new career move. It may mean several meetings working with the association or it may mean setting new expectations, and certainly it must be in conjunction with the district administration and probably the district's legal counsel.

Here are some certainties about removing an employee who has not reached the A level but hovers around the C.

It may be difficult, but it is possible.
It may take time, but the result is worth it.
It may cost money, but in the long run it will save.
It may take creativity, but that is good.
It should be a win-win for employee and school.
It will be a win-win for students and staff.

You Can Really Improve an Employee?

It's too often said that you can't improve or remove an employee. There are dozens of excuses available at times about why this won't work. It costs too much. There are too many legal hoops to jump through. They will sue you. It isn't the right thing to do for the employee. They will retire in a few years anyway so why bother? They aren't hurting anyone.

They are doing the best they can. Their heart is in the right place.

Here are my answers: An employee that prevents a system from providing the best opportunities for kids is costing kids a chance to learn. Hoops are made to jump through. Go through the process once and everyone will know you will do it again. You can be sued for anything, so why fear being sued for doing what is best for kids? You are here for the kids, not the employee. Every year that you give an employee a pass because they are close to retirement, or because they aren't hurting someone, or because they have a good heart is a year you deny a student the opportunity to get the best education you can provide.

Reality check: Most teachers are excellent. They sacrifice time and passion to make a difference. Most of them want the building and the system to be excellent. Most will support your reasonable efforts to make an employee do their best. Yes, you are here for the teachers and all employees but the purpose of the profession is to provide quality opportunities for learning—*for kids.* We can't escape our primary mission; we can only work hard to achieve it.

Termination is more of a choice than an act. Once you decide that you can't lead the employee any farther, that they are preventing the system from attaining excellence, that you have given remediation your very best effort, then make the choice to terminate and find a way.

The sooner you eliminate the employees not willing to do their best, the faster you move down the road of excellence. It's worth the work.

I once read an article that listed eight ways to live a life of purpose. It was adapted from the Marc and Angel Hack Life blog. Number seven reads: "Let go of what you don't need. Don't hold on to people, circumstances, and things that aren't bringing value to your life." I never forgot it. It makes sense for the principal especially when it involves holding onto weak employees who avoid improvement. Fix them or remove them.

The School Principal's Toolbook

The Law Is Changing

All across the United States new laws are giving administrators more flexibility and empowerment to remove tenured
teachers. Changes in the evaluation process are being tied to
student achievement, and that alters the entire process of
teacher improvement. Teachers who didn't take improvement
strategies seriously before are beginning to now. The use of
technology to assist evaluations, the expanded use of research
as a measure for teacher effectiveness, and the overall mindset
that tenure was never intended to protect weak teachers really
are causing a paradigm shift for teacher improvement and re-
tention. The Common Core movement, the digital revolution
(Zoom Learning), and a new focus on effective teaching are
evident everywhere. Principals now can make a case for a
teacher's improvement, remediation, or termination based on
test scores, student input, teacher involvement, and a vast list
of other inputs. Principals need to be aware of these opportunities and use them to insure that they have the best staff possible.

Summary

Building the best staff possible comes from all the steps
and ideas we have discussed. It is a process, and it may take
time, but it should be the goal and number one responsibility
of every administrator. This best sums it up:

I once read a story of an administrator who turned an entire school system around based on one thought "...fire them
up, or fire them."

Clay Ramsey says, "Hire good people and then let them be
good."

Margarit Spear adds, "If you want to create a lasting mas-
terpiece, you have to use quality materials."

Then there is the old Finnish proverb, "A rotting tree leans
long before it falls."

A last proverb, from China: "A speck of mouse dung will
spoil a whole pot of porridge."

So, hire excellent candidates, work your magic with the ones you inherited, and continue toward the goal of developing the best staff possible.

Chapter 5

Leading the Leaders

Leadership is like love. It comes in many forms and many styles. I do not love pizza like I love my wife. I certainly love my kids in a way that I can't really describe, but it has no relationship to how I love to watch *Survivor*. I guess the common core (excuse the term) is that love is a feeling, an emotion, a form of expression, but it comes in so many varieties that it is hard to describe.

The same is true for leadership. There are books (lots of them) written on the topic. I have read dozens. There are university classes dedicated to the understanding of leadership styles, the history of leadership, and how to lead.

Phil Blair, president of Manpower Staffing Services of San Diego, defines *leadership* this way: "Leadership is harnessing the energy and efforts of a group of individuals so that their outlook is advanced from an unremarkable Point A to a very desirable Point B, from bad to good, slow to fast, red to black. During that process, leadership manifests in projecting your expertise in a way that gains the confidence of others. Ultimately, leadership becomes about trust—when that confidence inspires them to align their vision and level of commitment for the betterment of the company." That, to me, is an amazing definition.

John Maxwell, a recognized guru of leadership, defines it simply as "influence." He also defines a leader as "one who knows the way, goes the way, and shows the way." Maxwell has written many books on the topic including *The 21 Irrefutable Laws of Leadership: Follow Them and People Will Follow You* and the *21 Indispensable Qualities of a Leader*. Those are just two of my favorites from a long list of his titles.

The definition of leadership goes from one word to practically a small book. So, for the purpose of the educational leader, what definition works best?

Honestly, I don't know. I say that because I don't believe leadership is something you can contain in a single universal definition. You certainly can describe some of its benefits, or list the anticipated results, or identify the qualities of being a leader, but to define it almost limits it. So let's consider a variety of opinions as we try to mold a leadership image. And, one hopes, along the way you will see some of the characteristics of leadership that have worked for you, and maybe because of you. That may help you put together your own leadership image, definition, or goal.

Leaders Are Innovators

Steve Jobs said, "Innovation distinguishes between a leader and a follower." To me, what he means is that leaders do not get squashed into compartments. They don't always follow prescriptive processes, or do things the same way time after time after time. If they did, they would be leaders of boredom, and in the educational profession boredom leads nowhere. Education is now laced with "Zoom," which means the wonders of technology. (I'll talk about "Zoom" later.) If a leader settles for mediocrity, that soon leads to stagnation. Thus, leaders need to innovate, inspire innovation, promote it, or allow it. Innovation means looking at things differently, and with excitement. Leaders also need to know how to weave innovation into successful standard operating procedures to make them exciting and productive at the same time. Innovative leaders must learn to measure the right amount of "newness" blended with the correct measure of "tradition," and shaken over a level of "comfort" so that frustration does not replace excitement.

Leadership vs. Management

Every school administrator has probably heard the old adage that leaders can manage, but managers can't always lead. There is some common sense to that statement if you think of leading and managing as two distinct actions. By one definition management "is the function that coordinates the efforts of people to accomplish goals and objectives using available resources." Leadership, however, is often considered a process where one person involves the *support* of others in the accomplishment of agreed-upon tasks. The difference in just about every comparison of management vs. leadership is the word "influence." To put it simply, and to make it very clear, *management is coordination; leadership is influence.* A good manager can certainly be a good leader, and a good leader certainly can be a good manager, but one *can* exist without the other. I can coordinate, motivate, organize, and reach agreed goals through management. I can do the same thing through leadership. However, if I lead you, *I help you accomplish a goal by influencing you.* If I manage you, I help you accomplish a goal, but not necessarily by influencing your thinking.

Without insulting your intelligence, let me give a very simple yet solid example. Suppose I tell you to go outside and keep the kids in line until the buses arrive, and when that task is completed you can go home. *This is management.* If I share with you the issue we have with kids trying to run between the buses to get to their rides, and the dangers that exist if kids aren't monitored, you now have ownership in the goal (safety). If I go one step farther and ask that you keep the kids in lines, tell you why we ask teachers to do this task (higher level of responsibility and trust), and I challenge you to think of a better way of keeping the kids safe while we help them board buses *and* get to their rides, I now have "managed" the situation, and hopefully caused you to understand the reason (building ownership), *and* challenged you to think of a better way (influenced innovation). *This is leadership.*

With that said, a great principal will always try to influence those he/she leads, changing them for the better while accomplishing the goals set before them.

Later in this chapter we will talk about some characteristics of good leaders. First, let's consider some leadership styles.

Classic Leadership Styles

When you went to college you likely studied three classic styles of leadership: autocratic, laissez-faire, and democratic. Hours were spent trying to analyze the benefits and evils of each. I can remember seeing examples of historic leaders listed under these headings, and taking surveys to determine where my style fit best—even before I had any style of my own. This exercise was like an aptitude test I took in high school that said I would become a farmer. A farmer?

To jar your memory, let's go back and review these classic styles of leadership.

The Autocratic Style of Leadership

The autocratic leader dominates team members, using unilateralism to achieve a singular objective. This approach to leadership generally results in passive resistance from team members and requires continual pressure and direction from the leader in order to get things done. Generally, an authoritarian approach is not a good way to get the best performance from a team or individual.

There are some times and situations where an autocratic style of leadership may be appropriate in schools. Some situations may call for urgent results, direct instruction, or corrective action. In these cases autocratic leadership may best fit the need. Some people may be most familiar with this type of leadership and have less trouble adapting to it since it is very prescriptive and may actually reduce the need, desire, or initiative to think or take risks. Tell me what to do, how to do it, and when and where, and I will not be responsible for the end result if I follow your lead. Some teachers and staff members may actually prefer this type of leader, but hopefully not the majority!

Laissez-Faire Leadership

Laissez-faire is French for "leave do." This type of leader exercises little control over his/her team, letting them sort out their roles and tackle their work, without the leader participating in the process. At times this can leave the team floundering with little direction or motivation. Of course there are degrees of laissez-faire leadership that do incorporate some overview, direction, and involvement of the leader, but in general, the "leave do" definition is true.

Once again, there are situations where this approach can be effective. If you have a team of highly motivated and exceptionally skilled people who have produced excellent work in the past, you may want to let them work on their own. And no matter what your initial style of leadership may be, there can be wisdom in stepping back and letting a confident, capable, and motivated group of teachers or staff members accomplish their task. In those cases when you hand over ownership you can empower your group to not only achieve but to go beyond just accomplishing the goals.

The risk that you take with laissez-faire leadership is when you lack capable and motivated personnel and the troops cannot accomplish the goals on their own. Fear, disappointment, discouragement, and, at times, raw anger can result.

Democratic Leadership

The third type of classic leadership is labeled "democratic leadership." The democratic leader makes decisions by consulting his/her team, while still maintaining control of the group. The democratic leader allows the team to decide how the job will be approached and who will perform which task.

Let's look at this from two perspectives. First, a democratic leader may encourage participation and delegate responsibility wisely, never losing sight of the fact that he/she bears the crucial responsibility of leadership. He/she values group discussion and input from team members, and often is seen as a person who draws from the strong points of the team in order to obtain the best performance and results. He/she motivates the team by empowering them to direct themselves but still guides them with a loose, but evident rein.

The second viewpoint, not as productive as the first, is that the democratic leader can also be seen as being so unsure of his/her leadership, and relationship with the team, that everything is a matter for group discussion and decision. Clearly, in this mindset, the leader is not leading at all.

Leadership Styles for Principals

Over the years there have been many styles of leadership suggested for principals. If you Google "leadership styles" you will see an abundance of titles and definitions. Many best fit business; some, clergy, and others, education.

In education, I've seen and tried lots of them, but I feel these five categories fit principals the best:

1. Manager Leadership

A manager leader is one who focuses on getting the job assigned and completed in the most direct and efficient manner. If the district mandates that teachers develop a common core curriculum that meets the parameters outlined on the handout given to them, the principal will organize the work, delegate the steps, set time lines, evaluate progress, and will expect a finished product at the time(s) specified. Here is what is needed, the date it is needed by, the directions or example, and the assignments to *"get 'er done."*

Another example is that the manager leader will work on the schedule for classes with input and parameters that he/she will mostly establish, may or may not involve a specialist, will distribute the product, and will make changes if needed.

What is lacking in this type of leadership is encouragement from the troops to think, to own, to participate in setting the goals, and to go outside the established boundaries.

The benefits? Some people like to be told, to have closed deadlines, and to operate on a directed, "managed" basis. It can be easier and less intrusive for the staff and team. Unfortunately these benefits come at the cost of innovation and creativity and a deeper satisfaction that comes from being inspired to think.

2. Inspirational Leadership

An inspirational leadership style can result in creativity and new ideas if the troops have the resources, direction, assistance, clear objectives, and ability. To just cheerlead is not enough, but some principals feel that their teams or staff can be inspired to fill in many of the blanks. We see inspirational leadership with motivational speakers or clergy who talk in generalities and leave their audiences moved or emotionally charged, but without specific guidance, tools, or skills to make the suggested changes. Motivational faculty meetings can do the same: leave a staff feeling great, but without true direction, equipment, or specifics to foster real growth. If leadership is influence, principals need to influence action, not just emotion.

The pros of this leadership are: (1) it sets a positive tone, (2) it may inspire short-term thinking, and (3) it helps build a positive environment. The cons are that without substance, direction, assistance, and evaluation, good intentions and expectations can fall flat.

3. Team Leadership

Many principals favor team building and team decision-making. This type of leadership tends to favor the laissez-faire model of hands off, letting the troops make the decisions. Good team building is a skill and is extremely useful when team decisions are desired. (We also have a chapter devoted to "teams" later in this book.) The capacity to build teams is a key factor in any form of leadership, but thinking that every decision, or even most, needs to be made by teams of teachers or other stakeholders is dangerous. When this type of leadership prevails it makes decision-making by the principal harder to accept, and even suspect. As well, if the principal does not agree with the team recommendations or direction, it can be quite awkward and sometimes divisive.

4. Pioneering Leadership

This relatively new leadership style comes from principals who take risks, push themselves and others, and are willing to go outside the norm to try new ideas. These types of leaders are both goal oriented and visionary. They are passionate leaders who see the goal and want to reach it. Their passion for making a difference can be catching and overwhelming. A good leader knows the difference. Pioneering leaders know what is working, know what needs to be improved, and plan for growth. They don't settle for the status quo unless it is helping to achieve the goals and visions.

This "new" form of leadership is both exciting and encouraging. There are few downsides unless the leader doesn't have the skills to bring everyone along and make the best use of teachers and staff.

Pioneering leaders are great at understanding the needs of the school and at setting the vision. But to really make a difference they need to develop strategic leadership skills...

5. Strategic Leadership

This is my favorite leadership style. I call this type of leadership "blended." Strategic leaders are able to take the best from all the other types, and know how to implement various strategies when needed. They can develop and encourage teams, they can be inspirational, they tend to cover the details without parking on them, and they seldom let minutia run the ship. They are "pioneering" in their attitude, passionate in their behavior, and visionary with every aspect of the job. But most important, they know how to implement the vision without taking control. Strategic leaders think about process, about the ability of their staff, about the need to set high expectations, about the vast benefits of developing ownership, and still are not afraid to insert some autocratic leadership when needed.

Strategic leaders are smart. Their knees are steady. They seldom suffer from knee-jerk reactionary behavior. They assess the people they work with, work for, and are responsible to. They can break a vision down into workable components (manageable chunks) and then craft a way to accomplish each step, utilizing teams, or individuals, or processes, or whatever fits the need. They are also respected for their work ethic and for treating everyone else with similar respect.

This type of leadership requires great skill and intuitive behavior. School leaders who display strategic leadership are often admired and respected, because they lead through well thought-out plans, they respect their staff, and they demonstrate a solid work ethic, blended with motivation and recognition along the way.

Developing Your Style of Leadership

How do principals develop their own style of leadership, and then how do they continue to improve? First of all, everyone needs to know who they are, what they do well, where they fall short, and how people respond to them. A clear assessment, done regularly, helps develop skills and make improvements.

My first years as a principal were interesting but probably not that different from most beginning building leaders recently transplanted from classroom to office. I had little practice, less training, and only a few years of teaching experience. I was thrown into the fire at a young age and had to learn quickly or sink. Every year, for several years, I asked my staff (certified and noncertified) to help me age gracefully by anonymously evaluating my effectiveness twice a year, *or whenever I needed it*. My first evaluation form was classic. It asked two questions: (1) If you could help me be a better principal and person, what would you change? and (2) List what you think we need to do in our building to better serve our students.

The first question was about me. The second question was about us. The whole idea of the "evaluation" was to focus on making me better, but also to think how "we" could be better. Guess what? It worked. I received some very helpful (never hurtful) responses. Only a few avoided the exercise, and they would probably have missed their own funerals. Most were extremely supportive. They knew I wanted to learn and become a better leader, and they helped me do it. I recognized something at a very young age that still helps me today, and that is one simple fact: *people who respect you want you to succeed*. Let me clarify that. You first have to earn their respect, and once you do, they are on your side!

During these evaluation exercises I even received a few suggestions that made me shudder and think, "I don't do that!" And then I really analyzed how I approached people, how they responded to my leadership, and I quickly realized, "That is *exactly* what I do!"

Another suggestion is to read. Read leadership books, study leadership examples, ask leadership questions. If you think something might be accomplished by trying a different leadership style, be honest and tell your staff you are trying something new and would like their input or opinion. Or try it first and then ask for an evaluation: "Did the process work?"

One of my favorite ways of finding my own successful leadership style was to ask the person who hired me or the one who evaluates me. If that is your superintendent or assistant superintendent, or principal if you are an assistant, ask that person for an *informal discussion*—not part of the formal evaluation. Simply say, "I'm trying to find the best style of leadership that meets the needs of my building and complements who I am. Will you help?" Ask them to tell you what style, attributes, or needs you currently have—without fear of your reaction—and grow from it. And remember, *their* leadership style may affect their response, so take that in consideration. You may want to lead differently, so be objective when asking for and receiving advice.

Leadership and Criticism

Leaders are always subject to review by anyone and everyone. Every decision, every response, every plan, every behavior is open for public and personal analysis. You can have the best leadership style on the planet and be an exemplary school leader, but you will never be immune to criticism or complaints.

So how does an exceptional leader handle criticism? First, what is criticism? It is the expression of a person's opinion, viewpoint, or observation about you, or about something you did, or even about something you said or the way you did it. Personal criticism is the hardest to accept because it is, well, *personal*. A well-trained leader is prepared for the unexpected and handles it with a well-planned reaction. Criticism is often imbedded in complaints. When anyone complains about what you did, how your team failed, your lack of leadership, your ignorance of what is going on, the quality of your staff, the unfairness of... (Go ahead, fill in the blanks!), they are usually blending a criticism in with the complaint. So let's talk about one of the most important skills a building leader needs to develop: how to handle complaints.

Accepting Complaints

I define "complaint" to include a wayward comment, a concern, a jab, a flat-out inflammatory outburst, or anything in between. It may come at a meeting, at the Dollar Store, at church. It may happen anytime or any place. Seldom do you have prep time so you need to be prepared 24/7.

Because school board members also attract complaints at the odd moments, in my book *The Art of School Boarding: What Every School Board Member Needs to Know* I outline how those members should accept (receive) a complaint, then how to respond to it (throw it back). It's equally applicable to principals and other leaders so let me share the process here through an acronym that should help you remember the steps used to catch (receive) the complaint. The acronym is CALM:

C-Compliment; A-Ask; L-Listen; M-Mimic

Compliment: The first step is to compliment the complainer! No matter how irritated they may be, or you may get, remember to compliment them. "Thanks for your interest in the school." "I appreciate your concern." "You have been a long-time supporter of the district, and that is appreciated." Get your compliment in to set the stage for what follows, always thinking of the word CALM. It will help you *stay calm* as you go through the steps. The compliment at the beginning may be the easiest step, and it is a way to focus your attitude, and theirs, in a positive direction. It may be very hard to do. You may only be able to say something like, "I understand it may be hard to share your concerns, but I am grateful that you are speaking directly to me."

Ask: As they discuss their concern, you will probably need to stop them and ask some questions. Your first question may involve the chain-of-command issue. With the building leader this is often the first question as well. Let's say the citizen is complaining about a discipline issue that they think was unjust.

Let's assume the disciplinary action was administered by a teacher, like having the child miss a recess for not turning in an assignment. After complimenting them, I would briefly listen to the initial complaint, then stop them and ask, "What did Nick's teacher say to you when you asked her about this issue?"

Do you see the direction I am suggesting? I am assuming the parent knows the proper chain of command and assuming she went there first. This is a much better approach than a back- sided reprimand such as, "You did talk to Nick's teacher about this, didn't you?" My first statement is factual and should not provoke controversy. My second statement is a put-down, with the assumption she didn't follow the chain of command. If the parent comes back with a sharp statement like, "No way am I going to talk to that teacher, we had her before when Sarah was in her class, and she was a pain then!"

Then you ask a follow-up chain-of-command question: "Okay, if you didn't talk to the teacher, then what did the assistant principal (or athletic director) say when you shared this concern with him/her?" Again, you are not offering judgment, just asking, what did you do about this issue before coming to me? Obviously, if you are the next person in the chain of command, this question is inappropriate.

Listen: Even if you want to defend the school, the teacher, the administration, or the nature of the beast in general, don't. Just listen with all the listening skills you can muster. Eye contact, no nodding because that might be construed as agreement, just maybe a comment if you need clarification. "Who is the person you just mentioned?" "When did you say this happened?" Questions should be asked only if you need more information when you indeed share this conversation, which you will, in most cases, even though the complainer will not expect that to happen.

Mimic: The last step in CALM is to mimic, or paraphrase. This is the final step before you begin to handle, or "throw," the complaint. Paraphrase means to summarize the comments if they need it, and in most cases, even if they don't. Here is an example: "Mary, let me see if I understand your concern clearly. Nick missed an assignment. You think it was his second or third missed assignment this term and Mrs. Hawken had Nick stay in during recess two days in a row to catch up with his missed assignment. You feel this is not an appropriate punishment. Do I understand your concern?" Expect the respondent to modify your summary, but keep to your plan. Stay CALM, don't encourage or engage in further discussion, don't agree, and unless you feel it is appropriate, don't even say you understand her concern or frustration.

If you have successfully "caught" the complaint, here is what you have done: You (1) started the conversation on a positive note by sharing a compliment, (2) suggested that the chain of command needed to be followed, (3) patiently, without interruption, listened to the story, and (4) summarized what you heard with a short and concise paraphrase, with no agreement or editorial comment on your part.

You have presented yourself professionally, positively, and with an attitude of concern. You also set up the next step by bringing the chain of command into the conversation. If you followed steps 1-4, calmly, you should be proud of yourself. It's not always easy to do, and in many cases, it takes practice.

Responding to a Complaint

Principals usually have two choices when they are given a complaint. They answer it because it is appropriate to do so, or they gently hand it back (throwing the complaint) with a sense of direction and assistance rather than compassion and understanding. If the complaint belongs somewhere else then that is where it must go, with some redirection from you.

If you need to "throw" the complaint, there are also four steps and a helpful word to remember: PASS. Pass infers to pass it off, and that is what you will do in many situations. PASS means:

P-Point; A-Avoid; S-Share; S-Summarize

Point: To "point" means to defer or refer. This is the tricky part. It is where you explain the chain of command to those who pretend not to know there is one. (Who doesn't know about the relationship between the boss and an employee? It's similar to the directions given on a plane—does anyone really need to be told how to fasten their seat belt?) You point the person to where they should go with the question or complaint. Yes, this is where they should have first gone and where they need to go now. Even if they tell you they don't want to go there, won't go there, or want to talk directly to the "head honcho," you gently indicate that policy requires that the person closest to the situation should be contacted first. Only if the problem can't be resolved, do you climb the chain. You also point out that in most cases problems are resolved quickly when the chain of command is followed. If they refuse to follow your guidance, pause for a moment. We will cover that later.

Avoid: Avoiding is very important. Avoid any promise of action. Avoid any assurance that you understand the issue. (In almost all cases, you can't understand when you only hear half of the problem.) And avoid a repeat of this situation by making it clear that the chain is the proper approach. Again, if they adamantly refuse to follow the chain, hold on for a moment.

Share: "Share" means to briefly share your role, your position in the chain of command, and your reliance on the system to function as designed. I would always tell them that if they go through the chain and are still not satisfied then you will certainly be glad to talk to them about ways to handle their concern. In some cases you will send them to the assistant superintendent, or even the superintendent. When you go above your level, you always offer to help them make the contact. You become very helpful, but you do not solve the problems when they aren't yours to solve. If you send them "down" the chain, and they refuse to go there, you offer to facilitate a meeting with all parties.

Summarize: The final S is for "summarize." I like this part. If done well, it ends the conversation on a win-win. If you have thrown the complaint to someone in the chain of command, and explained the why appropriately, you have done your job well. If you need to discuss the complaint with the person, and you do it calmly and respectfully and with the intention of finding the facts before you offer potential solutions, you will have done your job well.

You aren't quite done, though, when you have finished PASS. You need to email or call those involved. If you suggested the complainer contact a teacher, the superintendent, or another administrator, you need to report this conversation, even if you think it was resolved or too minor to be reported.

Your upward chain of command is probably to the superintendent (or principal if you are on the building team) so if you feel they need to be aware of the situation, be sure to email them an FYI as well.

Remember, when dealing with criticism, have a plan. Remain CALM, know the PASS technique, and when or where to use it, and always be fair and respectful. Golda Meir may have said it best, "You cannot shake hands with a clenched fist."

Comments About Leadership

W. Alton Jones once said, "The man who gets the most satisfactory results is not always the man with the most brilliant single mind, but rather the man who can best coordinate the brains and talents of his associates."

A leader influences, and that means somehow moving your team in the direction you feel is best as you make them the owners of the move.

It also means that at times you need to take the more difficult path, the more challenging routes, and you need to confront comfort. Mark McCormack says it this way, "(leading)... is a constant process of breaking out of systems and challenging conditioned reflexes, of rubbing against the grain."

We've talked a lot about ownership, and it is inherent in productive leadership. It is giving an idea to the team and somehow turning things around until they think they gave birth to it themselves. It is an incredibly productive skill. It takes finesse and it is not at all sneaky or underhanded. It is great leadership. You plant a seed and they grow it until they forget where the seed came from.

Harry Truman said, "It is amazing what you can accomplish if you do not care who gets the credit."

Another famous quip about leadership helps define one of the nuances of a being a productive leader. A famous Hungarian politician in the early 1900s by the name of George Mapir is the author of this quote, which is really a valuable leadership process: "When you must shoot an arrow of truth, dip its point in honey."

It may indeed be the foundation of a great book, which I feel should be mandatory reading for all school administrators, *The One Minute Manager* by Ken Blanchard and Spencer Johnson. (If you have never read or studied this book, download it, and read it. You will be grateful to learn the leadership skill they share.) The concept is simple: surround leadership with kindness and respect. The principle of one-minute managing is that you sandwich an order or a correction between legitimate compliments. Here is a good example of what I mean.

Let's say that John is one of your teachers. He was given a task by the head of the grade-level curriculum committee, Marian. The task is to secure some technology samples for the group to study as they work toward an improvement goal. John has not secured the materials and has offered lame excuses why. His lack of completing the task is holding back the progress of the group. Marian has come to you (the principal) for help. She is frustrated by the lack of ownership John has in the process and while others seem excited about what they are doing, John seems to care less. He is not responsive to Marian's requests, and Marian feels he may in fact resent her role as leader. Marian asks you to help get John onboard and keep the rest of the staff enthused. This is an opportunity for you to use your skills of strategic leadership, and implement the One-Minute-Management process.

You approach John after school the same day that Marian came to you. You have thought out your script, even rehearsed it a bit, before you enter the room. Here is what you say. "John, good to see you. I enjoy coming into your classroom since it always has an atmosphere of creativity and excitement. I love the evidence of kids working and the obvious use of technology that goes on in this room. I do want to drop by again soon and see you in action. You're a fantastic teacher.

"You're probably wondering why I stopped by. I understand you have had some delays in getting the technology information to the curriculum committee. I was talking to Marian about the progress and she said they are in a holding pattern right now. I know that everyone on the committee, myself included, is relying on your expertise to select the materials you feel are best for this project. You hold a key position in the direction we go, so it is imperative you feel good about the selections you make, which may influence learning for a long time. John, do you need some time off, maybe a half day to make calls or do your research? I think I can get a sub for you. I know the committee wants to meet the deadlines we all agreed upon and your work is really important. So, John, here is what I need. Let me know in the morning, before school, what your time line is and if I can help with a sub. If you think you might need a sub tomorrow, give Sue a call and tell her I authorized a half-day sub for you, but please call before 8 tonight. In either case, let me know before school tomorrow morning. Can you do this, John? Thanks. And, as Marian said, no one has the expertise to do this better than you do, and I agree. Thanks for serving on this important committee. I look forward to hearing from you and I will be in contact about coming in to see one of your great lessons soon."

No action is complete, no leadership process is successful, if you don't include follow-up or evaluation, so the first thing you do when you get back to your office is email Marian letting her know that you talked to John, and will have some progress to report tomorrow. Then go to your calendar and make a note for one week from today to email John about when he will be having one of his "action" lessons so you can drop in (as you promised).

Leadership is more than definitions and outlines. Leadership is action. How did you "lead" in the above example? You complimented a fine teacher, you instilled ownership by telling him he was crucial to the success of the program, you reminded him that the deadlines were agreed upon by everyone (not autocratically imposed), you talked about the goals (vision), you then broke up the expected response into manageable chunks (deadline), and offered resources (sub). You set the expectation, set the deadline, established the desired end product, and sandwiched everything between two real, heartfelt compliments. You dipped the arrow in honey, but still fired it!

Leadership is influence. Getting your staff and your constituents to work together willingly and eagerly to accomplish the mission is effective leadership.

Leadership is also leading by example. Solon B. Cousins puts it this way, "In believing in others, we are believed. In supporting others, we gain followers, and in recognizing the value of others, we are honored."

Leadership

We started this chapter by saying the obvious, that a precise definition of leadership is elusive. You can find a baker's dozen of them, you can list a myriad of leadership qualities, and you can build a leadership model customized a thousand ways. But there are certain basic fundamentals repeated again and again. We have mentioned many of them. A great leader never rises to the top by standing above his/her staff or by ordering them into submission. The leader rises to the top when the team rises and carries the leader along. Visions are brought to life when the team is the owner, when the group does the work, and when everyone believes in their worth. An effective leader causes all of these things to happen by respecting the value of the staff, by building consensus, and by transferring ideas from leader to constituent.

Still, as Dave Weinbaum says, "Sometimes you have to put your foot down to get a leg up." You don't build a strong school with a weak staff. You don't implement growth by avoiding decisions, or being too wimpy to make the tough ones.

Finally, good leaders build a top quality staff, with exceptional morals and strong character. Strength builds strength;

weakness permits weakness. To be a strong and effective leader, one must work at it every day, through every action, measured by every decision.

"Our rewards in life will always be in direct ratio to our service."

Earl Nightingale, author/speaker

Chapter 6

Change, Vision, and Motion

As you have already read on these pages, there are many types of leaders and many styles of leadership. I remember reading the following quote, that is also apropos: "Do not walk behind me, for I may not lead. Do not walk ahead of me, for I may not follow. Do not walk beside me either. *Just leave me alone!*" Guess what, that type of leader does exist! It's the type who says, "I don't care about change and I don't care about vision—because I don't care!"

But since you are reading this book, I am assuming you do care. You want to improve things and make a difference.

The title of this chapter includes the word "motion." Motion is the key to the success in change and vision. You see, you can sense or even know that there is a need for change. You can communicate a vision, but neither will happen without action.

Let me throw another concept into the mix. Failure. It is almost impossible to achieve anything without in some way tripping over failure. So we must talk about it too and see how it actually helps.

Assessing the Need

"There is no use waiting for your ship to come in unless you have sent one out." Nobody knows who said that but it could hardly be truer. You can't fix what you don't know is broken, nor can you change what you haven't yet made. A great many administrators float through their careers doing exactly those things. They wait to harvest excellence, but haven't planted any of the seeds. They hope that the new hires will make a difference, but they haven't identified what difference needs to be made. In other words, they float, unaware of any needs unless someone tells them about them. Then they become managers, or fixers, rather than leaders. Some principals let the superintendents aim the ship and plot the course and they're happy to take the ride. And if there's blame they'll give that to others too, not caring about the process enough to really get excited about it. *They just do what they are told.*

Let's hope this isn't you. Effective school leaders realize they are on the front lines. You know the ones who see and feel the needs. You should also have an inner clock telling you it is time to move, time to change, or time to grow. It becomes part of who you are, no matter your role. To a very large degree, you must keep your "scopes" clear and focused not just on your part of the system but on the whole system as well. In many cases the true leaders will move the entire system as they move their building, department, or area of responsibility.

The first, and possibly the most important, part of the process is the assessment of conditions, needs, progress, or achievement. Assessment of needs is as an extraordinarily broad statement because in the educational arena we could be talking about student achievement, teacher education, financial capacity, facility condition, attitude of staff, support of parents, community involvement, safety of the fleet, sales of food, safety of the playgrounds, lines of communication, or a thousand other measurable variables. Maybe ten thousand.

So how does the effective principal assess needs in the building?

* Test scores show achievement.
* Evaluations show staff effectiveness.
* Tardy numbers can show a number of things such as the effectiveness of passing-time changes or which classes kids are *not* excited to attend.
* Work order requests can indicate which custodians or maintenance staff members are least effective.
* Complaints from parents can point to teacher (or administrator) issues.
* Unrest among the employees can indicate morale problems or a lack of understanding of certain policies.
* Recorded down time on technology equipment can flag a need for newer equipment, better repair and maintenance programs, or improved instruction on operation skills.

The School Principal's Toolbook

* Kids getting unusual numbers of detentions can indicate teacher discipline effectiveness or the need for character education programs.
* Unusual crowdedness or an increase in fighting in certain parts of the building can flag a facility issue.

In most of these examples data was used to indicate a need. Counting the number of incidents, keeping track of complaints, analyzing test scores, calculating expenses compared to projections. Assessment comes in a variety of forms and at times the assessment numbers are already there, you just need to see them, count them, and analyze them.

Another way of analyzing need is by asking your team to brainstorm or discuss what is trending. At faculty meetings, during informal conversations, whenever the group assembles, extend an invitation to share actions or incidents that seem to be occurring, or are growing in magnitude, or are vanishing... Those kinds of discussions are great ways to analyze quickly and efficiently.

There is another way the leader can assess needs—and it's quite simple. Just look and ask. Watch what is happening and ask why. If the principal sees that this year's test scores in middle elementary math are dropping, you needn't bring in the troops from Harvard. Assemble the math teachers, present the evidence, and let the providers ponder the question. If you aren't pleased with the response, do more investigation. "That class isn't very bright, so the scores are lower," they say. That may be true, but if you dig deeper and find that the same class of kids functioned better last year or two years before, you may have some doubt that "class brightness" is the real reason. And even if it is, doesn't the assessment of declining scores still warrant a review of teaching techniques needed to meet the needs of this class?

Your staff also needs to understand that any needs assessment you initiate, or ask them to help complete, is not a witch hunt but a fundamental first step in making improvements. If you have a wing of your building that seems to be dirtier than the other wings, the assessment can be more of a question than an indictment. Why does hallway C always look messier than hallway B? The result may be that there is twice the traffic in hallway C, thus it may be necessary to switch some of the workload of the hallway B custodian to help the hallway C custodian. No indictment of effort, but an improvement in procedure. If it turns out that the hallway C custodian is just inept or failing to follow the correct procedures, that too can be fixed.

When I arrived as the new principal I was told that one section of my building was hotter in the winter than the other rooms—and the teachers that taught there just accepted it, figuring, I guess, that it was because the building was old. In winter they would open windows to balance the temperature. I'd written it on my clipboard but that's where it hid. (My clipboard then was to me what my phone "notes" app is today.) Fortunately I was reminded of it again by a community member at a Lions Club meeting. He was new to the community too, so he wondered why the windows would be open when it was freezing outside.

I guess it had been written off since the teachers didn't complain nor did the maintenance department.

When I returned to school from the Lions Club meeting, rather than writing out a work order I went directly to the maintenance department and talked to the man responsible for the boilers. I asked him why these rooms were so hot since they were in the middle of the steam line (not closest to the boiler, nor the farthest). He said, "They've always been hotter. It must be a design defect."

I didn't buy the design defect. Anyway, we were heating the outside all winter—on the school budget! My "needs assessment thinking" made me wonder what was up, since my expectation was that every classroom should be educationally appropriate, comfortable for learning, and efficient in terms of cost of operation.

So I went back to my office and called a plumber to see if, off the cuff, he had any idea why there was a heating discrepancy in that school wing. "Sure," he said. "Probably the valves in that part of the building aren't closing like they should." Bingo. A quick check showed that the valves in these rooms hadn't been inspected, cleaned, or replaced since the day Eve bit into the apple. One overdue question and a simple solution helped us take a bite in our utility bill and replaced the status quo attitude that "that's the way it's always been."

Why Are They Tardy?

Here's another but very different needs assessment story. It relates to the assistant high school principal who was asked to fill out a time line of his daily activities.

The new superintendent asked each administrator to do this task. The assignment couldn't have been more direct: write down a typical work routine on a "normal" student-attendance day. In other words, how much time do you spend fulfilling your responsibilities?

When the results came back the superintendent sat down with each building principal to review each survey, asking questions such as "Does this report fit the perceived job assignments?" "Does this work routine help achieve the mission?" (assuming they had one and understood it) and "Does this schedule move the building or district forward?"

It turned out to be an extremely productive and worthwhile activity. When the time line of one assistant principal was reviewed, it showed that between 75 and 90 minutes each morning, after first hour ended, was spent processing student tardy notices. This seemed like an inordinate amount of time considering the number of students and the high attendance rate of the school. The principal said that he needed to do some homework based on this information. He went to the assistant principal and asked to see the data on first-hour tardy reports. "Data?" he asked. "You mean something besides the number of kids tardy each day?" The principal was surprised. Obviously the school had never dissected or discussed the tardy numbers, it just responded to them individually by student. Who knew?

The principal suggested that for the next few weeks the assistant collect some additional data. Create a chart with the student's name, grade level, teacher who reported them, and maybe a reason posted for the tardy, plus anything else that might be of interest. The assistant said, "No problem, easy to do."

The principal marked her calendar to ask the assistant about the data in three weeks. When the time came the assistant was almost jubilant with the results. "Do you know that over 25% of my tardies come from the same teacher? I can't believe it!" The principal and the assistant sat down and discussed why. Their answer, based in part on knowing the quality of the teacher, was that kids were not excited about getting to her class. The teachers that most kids respected and appreciated had occasional tardies, but this teacher had by far the most on a regular basis. The needs assessment turned up valuable data, and from it the administrators developed a needed vision, that tardies would be reduced. The vision necessitated a change, and that resulted in action.

In case you are wondering, a conference with the teacher was held and she was informed of the percentage of tardy students she reported and that it might be related to the way she started the class, the excitement of the class, or the desire of students to get to the class on time. Of course this caused an intense discussion that resulted in ways to investigate and fix the causes. She was also told that while she was working on the problem there would be discussions whenever a student was tardy in order to determine why and what reasons were given   until the administration and teacher could find or develop a remedy. This did not involve discipline or change of work conditions or anything contrary to the professional agreement, only an attempt to improve the attendance of kids. Those caused the teacher to improve and the number of tardies to decline.

Vision

The Reverend Theodore Hesburgh once said, "The very essence of leadership is that you have to have a vision. It's got to be a vision you articulate clearly and forcefully on every occasion. You can't blow an uncertain trumpet."

What comes first—improvement, change, assessment, or vision? Well, in many organizations any one of these might come first. Emergencies might prompt immediate change without a vision or a needs assessment. A vision might cause a leader to do a needs assessment to calculate what change is needed to fulfill the vision. A vision might result from some change that came from the outside and now has kick-started a new look at what might be down the road. So the honest answer is that in real life, the vision might not dictate the change. However, that does not trump the fact that good leadership is visionary, and great leadership knows how to implement a vision successfully.

What Is Vision?
It might be the ability to see something you want to happen. It's also a thought, concept, or object formed by the imagination. Put these together and you get my definition of a vision. The ability to see something not there *but needed*. A visionary is a person who creates a vision. Yet an administrator who makes a difference adds one more element to the equation. He/she not only creates a vision, but also *has the ability to articulate it.*

Let's set some conditions to the role of visionary. In order to really create a vision you need to be able to set aside limitations. You need to go beyond what is sometimes practical and affordable, and you need to reach beyond the constraints of everyday operations. Imagination should never be limited by restrictions. Reality will come in the implementation, but if it tempers the dream, then the vision is tainted to start with.

If my vision of an excellent school includes teachers who *all* perform at the "Exceeds" level, all earn A evaluation scores, and all are cooperative and influential in moving the school forward, then that becomes my focus. Might it never happen that I have 100% near-perfection on my teaching staff? Should I aim for something less, thinking that my goal or vision is too high? Is it possible that someone might say this is unrealistic and a foolish target? Well, since I'm not brain dead, I know that this vision might never reach 100% fulfillment, and I know that some may consider it a foolish venture, but what is a vision if it isn't reaching beyond the expected? And is it okay to have a vision that 80% of your teachers are the best? No, it's not, because that says it's acceptable to have teachers who fail, teachers who don't meet standards of excellence.

So a vision should be far reaching, even sometimes reaching into the "hard if not impossible to accomplish" zone.

Brian Tracy once said, "Imagine no limitations; decide what's right and desirable before you decide what's possible."

Visions can also be more short-termed and more quantitative. A principal might have a vision that the school will be a place where students and staff experience an environment conducive to learning 24/7. This vision might address a building that is well lighted, comfortable in temperature, with appropriate seating, clean everywhere, and staffed with exceptional people and up-to-date equipment. A vision like this, that is well articulated and shared, might begin a process that is extremely comprehensive, that beckons ownership, and welcomes ideas for implementation. It might even be dissected into several smaller visions like a vision dealing with the facility, a vision focusing on staff, and another emphasizing equipment. One vision may become three, or more.

There are no rules for visions, only thoughts and ideas of how to give them value.

Here are some additional thoughts on the concept of visions:

* "What would life be like if we had no courage to attempt anything? (Vincent Van Gogh)
* "Act locally, but think globally." (Rene Dubos)
* "We must not be afraid of dreaming the seemingly impossible if we want the seemingly impossible to become a reality." (Vaclav Havel)
* "There is a bigger picture, just step back from the canvas." (Ilona Simone)

Who Owns the Vision?

"Big thinkers are specialists in creating positive, forward-looking, optimistic pictures in their own minds and in the minds of others," says David J. Schwartz

The key to successful visionaries, as stated above, is their ability to articulate their vision. Let's go a step farther, because although the articulation of the vision is essential, just as important is transferring the ownership of the vision. My vision needs to be your vision if you are going to have the passion to make it happen.

Imagine a leader standing before his staff and outlining his vision for the high school. "I'd like to have every student leave here a contributing member of society, all able to swim, and each having scored 30 or more points on the ACT exam." Lofty goals. Loftier yet if the school has no swimming pool. The staff may whisper, "Has he gone daft?" They may also think, "Some of these goals are reasonable," or "Where is he going with this?"

But what if some time passes and the staff begins to consider that a character education program might indeed help students learn aspects of being a contributing member of society. And they then discuss that indeed there is a huge need for kids to learn to swim since the area has numerous lakes. And they also realize that because the academic program is exceptionally strong, high ACT scores are possible. The staff members might begin to think that the vision is not so strange after all! In fact, if the leader were to assemble the staff, steer the discussion in such a way that *they want character education, that providing a pool would meet the needs of the kids, and they could easily be one of the strongest educational schools in the area*, then, in fact, they might even begin to take ownership of this vision themselves. When that happens *it becomes theirs and not the leader's.* A good leader can introduce topics, then share ownership with others, to collectively develop the vision.

I remember once when an administrator wrote down a vision to build a new school within a certain time frame to meet the needs of more space, improved learning environment, better technology, and increased athletic opportunities. Instead of sharing this well-thought-out vision (that even included the location, grade levels, and financing), she started conversations with various segments of the community and staff, stressing needs, listening to concerns, accumulating evidence, and even *steering* ideas about solutions, until the end result was a community-staff proposal for, guess what, a new middle school. The vision was theirs, but the seed to grow the vision was planted by her. That is what makes a vision successful, having others take ownership from early on.

Hyman Rickover once said it like this, "Good ideas are not adopted automatically. They must be driven into practice with courageous impatience."

Planting the idea for a vision takes time and good planning. It also takes great patience. Vision creating is easy. Designing the structure and transferring ownership of a vision is not. When people start to take ownership and show passion for the needed changes or improvements, that is when you may need to step up and help *them* formulate *their* vision. When that happens, half the battle has been won.

Fear and Failure

Creating the vision, transferring the vision, even giving the vision some form all take a certain level of courage. No one wants to look like a dunce and no one wants their ideas to be made fun of or to look half-witted. Even to introduce a need such as "all kids need to know how to swim to graduate" when there is no pool may look crazy, but if the reasons are sound they might also look brilliant. Alas, it takes great courage to avoid looking crazy. And since courage is the absence of fear, a good leader cannot be afraid to fail.

"I failed my way to success," said Thomas Edison. Although he never really invented the light bulb, it took him two years and reportedly 6,000 tries to create an incandescent light that would last. He is also credited with inventing hundreds of light bulbs that would never light. He is reported to have said that every one of this experiments that failed was really a success because it taught him what not to do.

The same is true for the principal. If a vision or an idea fails it provides a learning experience to build from.

John Maxwell has a book entitled *Failing Forward*. In it he gives 15 steps to failing forward, which simply means learning from the inevitable failures a great leader will encounter. Here are the 15 steps:

1. Realize there is one major difference between average people and achieving people.

The School Principal's Toolbook

2. Learn a new definition of failure.
3. Remove the "you" from failure.
4. Take action and reduce your fear.
5. Change your response to failure by accepting responsibility.
6. Don't let the failure from outside get inside you.
7. Say good-bye to yesterday.
8. Change yourself, and your world changes.
9. Get over yourself and start giving yourself.
10. Find the benefit in every bad experience.
11. If at first you do succeed, try something harder.
12. Learn from a bad experience and make it a good experience.
13. Work on the weakness that weakens you.
14. Understand there's not much difference between failure and success.
15. Get up, get over it, and get going.

Maxwell's in-depth explanation of each of these steps will change your perspective on failing.

Over the years working with outstanding leaders I have learned that fear and failure can defeat or strengthen you. Failure is not avoidable, nor is it life defining, unless you let it be. Failure, it's said, is the greatest teacher.

Once early in my teaching career I recall spending a great amount of time preparing what I considered to be a wonderful lesson for a bunch of perspiring and hormonally challenged eighth-graders. I couldn't wait to present it. About 20 minutes into the class they looked like they were ready to hide in a casket. They were dozing, yawning, and bored to death. I realized that the entire lesson plan was one step short of misery. Instead of accepting that this was a failure, I ended the lesson plan, then asked everyone to take out a piece of paper and write down three ways that the lesson could have been made more interesting. I told them that this was their homework for the day, and it was okay to talk with their neighbors before writing down their ideas.

Modestly, that was nothing short of on-the-spot genius! I studied their responses that night and changed the way I taught from that day forward. I took a flop and flipped it to a home run. The very next day I injected some of their ideas into my teaching, giving them credit and thanking them for teaching me.

I've never stopped that process. When something didn't work, I tried to find out why and learn from it. After all, we are in the learning business! As a principal I did the same thing after faculty meetings. Several times, particularly when I was first finding my way, I ended the meeting with a short survey that they turned in as they left. Here were the three questions on the survey: "Concerning this meeting, (1) What worked? (2) What didn't? (3) How would you do things differently?" These types of "learning opportunities" were absolutely enlightening and helpful. They still are! I read every single evaluation from the administrator academies I give today—they are my best teachers. When I fail to meet someone's expectations I want to know why and then learn how to do it better the next time.

Depending on your attitude and preconceived disposition, fear, failure, and problems can either be discouraging or encouraging. Norman Vincent Peale, a renowned clergyman and prolific author, said it this way, "There is only one group of people who don't have problems and they're all dead. Problems are a sign of life. So the more problems you have, the more alive you are."

Another great quote comes from the inventor Charles Kettering. In a speech where he pointed out that you can learn how to fail intelligently, he said, "Once you've failed, analyze the problem and find out why, because each failure is one more step leading up to the cathedral of success. The only time you don't want to fail is the last time you try."

Tim Storey, a well-known religious leader, says "If you have a setback, don't take a step back—get ready for the comeback."

Finally, a Japanese proverb says, "Fall seven times, stand up eight."

Change

Terry Heick wrote an article for teachthought.com entitled, "The Ed Reform Ninja: 8 Sneaky Strategies For Change In Your School." It's a great article and I greatly appreciate the eight "strategies" he lists. I've taken the liberty of slightly converting his steps into a list of considerations for administrative change, and have added some observations of my own.

1. Start small
This means to break the change you want into manageable chunks, a size that you can accomplish and measure. Start quietly without a lot of fanfare. Make the changes meaningful, yet manageable from the beginning.

2. Forget about policies
In the beginning, focus on the change itself, disregarding sweeping policy revisions, legalities, or politics. If you see the change is possible and workable, those other things will fall into place at the right time. Don't be foolish, however.

3. Know whom to avoid
I love this step because it really means avoiding the person, people, or group who will say no without trying. They will focus on the obstacles, not the vision. You may need to provide some evidence before the naysayers come on board.

4. Pick your battles
We talk about this a lot in this book. In almost every situation where leadership makes a difference, effective leaders don't fight battles that aren't theirs nor seek battles to prove a point. They carefully ask the question, "Will this battle help me win the war, or will it just take up time?" Or, "Is this my battle to fight, or do I need to transfer ownership of this battle to others?"

5. Don't start a clique
Good leaders involve the entire team. Closed-focus leaders only involve the doers or the high achievers and thus fail to de-

velop all team members. Develop ownership and build morale at the same time. It is easy to go to those who will support your ideas or make progress quickly, but this can be a fatal mistake. Seek out the strengths of everyone and get each person involved in one way or another.

6. Honor disagreement
If disagreement allows for honest communication, the transfer of constructive ideas, and an opportunity to look at more sides than you present, go there. If disagreement is just for the sake of argument, be polite but don't get drawn into this obstruction of progress.

7. Start now
We are going to visit this in greater detail in a few pages because it is one of the most important ingredients of excellent leadership. If you wait for "*the planets to align*," as Terry says, you may miss the target. Go for it sooner than later. Be prepared, be excited, have a plan, and move.

8. Work to eventually grow your team
I love Terry's explanation "*If you want to go fast, go alone; if you want to go far, go together.*" If you want to implement change, start small, build on successes, grow ownership, transfer the ideas from you to them, let them "feel" the need and "see" the possibilities, then let them run, with you standing aside, but always in the lead.

Watch the Pendulum

The old will become the new, and the new will reflect the old. When the pendulum switches from this idea to that, or when "new" reform seems to mirror "old" reform, understand that all change reflects where we have been and moves to where we want to go, and somewhere along the way we rediscover that where we have been may not really need to be entirely reinvented.

Let me share a message from Eric Casarotto, assistant headmaster at Kuper Academy. He says, "Our school has a no cell phones in the class policy. Students, however, are permitted to use these during their time—recess and lunch. At first one would look at rows of tables of students busily texting, updating their Facebook, tweeting, and all sorts of things that as a middle-aged man I find strange and somewhat exotic. Well, we installed two ping-pong tables and two foosball tables in the cafeteria as well as opened up a board-game room at lunch. All of a sudden, the vast majority of students are socializing in a healthy manner. Few are still tethered to their smart phones... Is the pendulum of revolution swinging back?"

Indeed, old ideas can be revisited, revamped, reworked, and reintroduced, and no one should ever oppose this. A great administrator knows that the pendulum from idea to idea swings back and forth. A great educator knows that research-based teaching and the fundamentals of good communication skills are never replaced by technology or paperless information. Taking from the best and transferring it into new and better applications is an art, not "old business."

Finally, it was Margaret Mead who may have said it best about change, "Never believe that a few caring people can't change the world. For, indeed, that's all who ever have."

Do It. Make It Work.

Assessments, ideas, the need for change, and building a vision, they all seem like precursors for action, and indeed they are. *You can't hit a target if you don't have one clearly in sight.* We need to add another component to this statement. *And, you can't hit the target if you don't take action.*

Hyman Rickover, the famous admiral, said, "Good ideas are not adopted automatically. They must be driven into practice with courageous impatience." The key words are "they must be driven."

And, you don't have to work fast, you just have to keep working. There is an old Colombian proverb that says, "With patience and saliva the ant swallows the elephant."

It took me eight years to see a new school built in the last district where I was privileged to serve. I started the process one month after I arrived in the district, and carefully, through failures and successes, helped build ownership, support, need, and a clear vision. I was able to transfer the vision from my head to the heads and hearts of hundreds of people. Over time, little by little, the vision became reality. It took a lot of patience, perspiration, and planning. Along the way three building referendums were defeated, and it seemed like failure would rise above success, but the day after each failure, the troops were rallied and the new effort began. The fourth and fifth referendums were overwhelmingly approved and all the hard work was paying dividends. During the process I was given a slip of paper with a quote from George Halas, "Nobody who ever gave his best regretted it." Hard work, sticking to the plan, keeping the faith, and focusing on the vision: these are the elements that garner success.

There are some basics to getting ideas transformed into action. In its simplest form, here are the steps.

1. Articulate the Needs and Vision
2. Construct the Plan
3. Break the End into Manageable Chunks
4. Evaluate, Adjust, Congratulate, Motivate
5. Never Finish

Articulate the Needs and Vision
If you have done a needs assessment and then crafted your vision for the future, then the very first step in getting things done may be the hardest: it is the transfer of data and vision into an understandable platform. This means that you move from data and goals into ownership and teamwork. You make your idea, or the ideas that have been developed by others, into an action plan based on passion and drive. Leadership is essential at this step. It is up to you to make sure everyone who needs to be involved understands the task, the journey, and the steps necessary to reach the goal.

Construct the Plan
Try to build a building without a plan and you will build a mess. Try to change the mindset of teachers without thinking through the details and, well, good luck. Try to do something

that raises taxes or moves money from one set of owners to another without buy-in, and maybe you should find a travel agent. A plan is absolutely essential to anything if success is the goal. The thing one needs to understand, however, is the plan can be general in nature and not lock-stepped in specifics. It can be fluid and developed as you progress. And, it needs to be a plan that you can compartmentalize into "manageable chunks."

Break the Plan into Manageable Chunks

Let's say your plan is to have a staff of educators second to none. This is a healthy vision for any administrator. Let's say you have 50 staff members on your team. You have identified 27 of them as top-notch, leading educators. Your assessment (formal and intuitive) has identified 18 more as B level educators. That leaves five who are, in your estimation, average or less.

Where do you begin the process? In my perspective it is with the five. If I am developing a plan I want it to be doable. Working with five teachers to bring them from average to excellent is going to be formidable, remembering that I have 18 others who still need to go from B to A as well. So why not start with one of the five, get him/her on board, then a second, and a third—all "on board" by the end of the first semester? Once this "chunk" of the plan (or five chunks) is off the ground, I may have the energy and resources to start a plan on the group of 18, and I may have grown my team of "workers" to tweak and build the plan as I go. See the thinking here?

Evaluate, Adjust, Congratulate, Motivate

That seems like four steps, but not so. All along the process you measure how it is going and make adjustments as needed. No plan is perfect from the start. When it is working you congratulate those responsible and inspire them to keep up the good work. When I was involved with the vision of a new school I can say that almost daily I did all four of these important actions. At the end of the day I would think about what was accomplished. On some days it would be nothing, and that was okay if I knew why and when we would be back on track.

The School Principal's Toolbook

If one "chunk" of the process was faltering while another "chunk" was moving rapidly, I did the evaluation, reassessment, and revision to the one and the "congrats and keep it up" with the other. This becomes part of who you are and how successful your efforts become.

At those times when I felt the plan was standing still, or even worse, dead, I reminded myself of the quote from Chuck Yeager, one of the world's best aviators, "You do what you can for as long as you can, and when you finally can't, you do the next best thing. You back up, but you don't give up." Maybe this is called self-motivation.

I received some personal motivation after a failed referendum. It was our third, and we lost by only a handful of votes after a very well-organized and hard-worked campaign. We were extremely disappointed. When I arrived in my office the next morning there was a rock on my desk, one of those composite rocks with an inscription that read, "Never, Never Quit." To this day I don't know who put it there. We didn't quit, and the next referendum won easily. The day after that victory I found a second rock on my desk. This one read, "Real leaders are ordinary people with extraordinary determination." Both of these meant the world to me. They still do. I can see them right now.

Never Finish

An old Chinese proverb says, "The person who says it cannot be done should not interrupt the person doing it." Another proverb, this from Japan, says, "Vision without action is a daydream. Action without vision is a nightmare."

No plan ever ends. There is always room for improvement, always a new technology, and for sure, *always* a new government initiative. No teachers reach their capacity—nor does the principal. Improvement plans never end, they just get reassessed, rewritten, fit into a new vision, and then re-upped for action. The administrator who says, "Done!" is fooling him or herself. There is no "done." So get prepared for creating a vision (no matter how limited or how vast), working toward its full implementation, only to have it modified or replaced by a newer and better one.

In Summary...

Let's admit that there are administrators who only react to the diaper philosophy, if something stinks we need to change it. And there are those who operate a school the old way, focusing on the traditional basics of "reading, writing, and arithmetic," failing to consider the three C's, as taught by Fred Gluck: "computing, critical thinking, and change." Then there are those administrators who think that things will change by themselves, failing to realize what Henry David Thoreau so majestically wrote, "Things do not change; we do."

That is the crux, the bottom line, the summation of this chapter: if we are to process a vision, if we are to see the need for assessment, if we are to champion change then *we must change*. We must be on the edge of what is new and what works. We must be ready and willing to challenge was is mediocre, and we must have the courage to face fear and failure knowing that they are teachers and not tyrants. We must see beyond today and look toward a future vision. We must set lofty goals, and those equally as important, but maybe not as glorious. The education of our kids truly rests in the ability of the administrator to change and thus facilitate change: to see, and thus open the window for others to see, and to switch the excitement from within to the hearts and souls of those who teach.

"I'd rather be a failure at something I enjoy than be a success at something I hate."

George Burns, actor/comedian/writer

Chapter 7

Communications

When I address college classes of students studying to be teachers, or even graduate classes of administrators, I am frequently asked what I think is the most important skill for an administrator. I tell them, without hesitation, it's the ability to communicate. Without a doubt this separates good from great. But to stop there is of little help to the principal-to-be. Communication needs to be defined and discussed, because it entails so many important and changing elements.

Think back and remember how your parents communicated with you when you were growing up. My parents communicated with me by holding me, changing me, talking baby talk to me, and even making funny faces at me—and that was when I was in my twenties! You get the idea. As we go from babyhood to adolescence our parents communicate differently, in different styles, using different methods, and today, using different devices. And when you go from adolescence to adulthood you start communicating with them differently too!

The days of the long letter or preplanned phone call are over. I remember my mom writing letters to me when I was in college and setting a time when I could call home, because there was one phone per floor in the dorm and you almost needed an appointment to use it. (In fact, we had a log by the phone and we would block out times for our calls, hoping that others would respect the request.) Now, your pocket vibrates, or as my wife's phone is doing this very minute, announces a call with the Beach Boys' version of "Barbara Ann" (her name). The need to communicate doesn't change but the way we do it changes almost daily.

Know Your Audience

I like to read and learn. I love books on leadership. I even love the ones that are quirky and offer different viewpoints. *The Leadership Secrets of Santa Claus: How to Get Big Things*

The School Principal's Toolbook

135

Done in Your Workshop...All Year Long is a fun book with a great message. *Jesus CEO* and *Lincoln on Leadership* are classics. One of my favorites is *My Personal Best* by John Wooden. But a book I bought by the dozens was *The Greatest Salesman in the World*, by Og Mandino. When I served as high school principal I used to give each graduating senior a copy of this book as a personal gift. Every one of the books I just mentioned, and shelves of more, have taught me something about how to communicate. Each of the authors and each of the characters and each of the stories, in some way, are based on communication skills.

When you study what works for others, you learn what might work for you. You begin to hone your own style. A book I recently read was, again, from the author John Maxwell, who is quoted often because I relate to his fundamental approach, his solid faith, and the way he shares his thoughts. He teaches with clarity, speaking in understandable words, and eliciting a message that comes as much from the heart as the head. He wrote a book called *Everyone Communicates, Few Connect*. This is an excellent book. John outlines a message I have long been telling my audiences, my students, and anyone who would listen. The message is very simple: know your audience and communicate in ways they best understand. A simple thought, but often overlooked.

When I give a sermon at a church, I write differently than I do when I prepare a paper for a professional journal. The setting, the intent, and the environment set the tone for both the audience and the presenter. When I speak to audiences of teachers and administrators I speak differently than when I am talking to parents and the general public, or students for that matter. Each audience has a different knowledge base, a different set of needs, and listens in its own unique way. When I write a letter to legislators I tend to write in a more fundamental fashion knowing that few politicians understand all the acronyms and terminology specific to every subject and every segment of society. You must slow down and give a more elementary outline of the topic than if you were talking to the state principals administrative association. Seems logical and without need to mention, doesn't it? And yet not formatting the communication appropriately is one of the biggest mistakes most administrators make. This doesn't suggest talking down or talking up, it means talking a language and in a style your audience understands.

To know your audience means to think like they do. That means asking them if they understand, if the message was clear, if you were too detailed and complicated or too simple and understated. Getting a read on your communications helps you do better the next time. A good speaker can "read" the audience and switch gears midstream if plan A is not working. A teacher needs to do the same, and a school administrator's success rate is directly related to the effectiveness of his/her communication ability. Talk to a single teacher, a team of teachers, the entire staff and if they don't get it or they walk away confused or angry or bored or misunderstood or feeling left out, you lose, and you lose big time. Knowing your audience and considering all the elements of this chapter are huge in becoming a highly effective administrator.

You Care, They Forgive

At a recent meeting one of the participants made a statement that really made an impression. We were talking about a young leader we were mentoring. He struggles at times by being "zoned out" when he passes by some of those whom he leads. His problem is no different than the principal who walks through the cafeteria with about 536 items on his mind. His immediate aim is to get to a classroom and talk to a teacher and in the process he doesn't take into account that he is passing a half-dozen other teachers eating at a table, one supervisor, and 200 kids, not to mention several cafeteria workers, all part of his "kingdom" and all who want to be greeted or at least acknowledged with a smile, grunt, or some form of human utterance. But this time he looks at no one as he walks through. He has a void expression on his face, and as soon as he passes by, many will comment. Some may realize that he "seems focused on something else," some may be less forgiving about his aloofness, and some may utter a negative comment about his total avoidance. No points were made, when a simple smile, a quick "how are you doing?" or a one-second stop to say something pleasant or appreciative would have made huge points on the positive side of the ledger.

There is a quote by Gabriel García Márquez that comes to mind, "The heart's memory eliminates the bad and magnifies the good; and thanks to this artifice we manage to endure the burdens of the past." In essence, you erase the negative stuff when you replace a bad act with a good one.

So, if the principal on his return trip through the cafeteria stops at the teacher's table and says, "I was so intent on my meeting that I walked through the cafeteria a few minutes ago and forgot to say hi or even appear alive! How are you all doing?" When people know that you care, they forgive a multitude of minor faux pas in your behavior. This is a great thing to remember as you try to build an effective communication armory. When you miss the target, go back and try again.

Connect

Maxwell shares four components of connection: connect visually, intellectually, emotionally, and verbally. *If you can connect to your audience*, whether it's one-on-one, in a newsletter that is sent to hundreds (and will last forever), or to an audience of ten or a thousand, *you will make a difference*. To connect means to engage, to strike a chord, to leave them with more than you found them with. It means that somehow you were able to capture their attention and, as Jobs said, "dent the universe." If you say or express something monumental or something incidental, if it relates to their needs or emotions, or makes an impression on their intellect, or simply causes them to think, then you have been a successful communicator.

Are all communications important? *Yes.* Even the communications that happen in passing are important. Even the ones that are well planned, double-checked, and printed on fancy paper are important, even though they may simply announce a date or time. So are the ones that are informal and happen on the go. Why? I remember an instructor when I was back in graduate school who frequently shared this quote, "What you are speaks so loudly that I can't hear what you say." Ralph

Waldo Emerson said that. Your very being is part of your communication no matter how formal, informal, planned, or instantaneous.

Before we get into the nitty-gritty, we need to remind ourselves that real communications are nothing more than an extension of ourselves, if they are authentic and true. You may write something and have others proof it, tweak it, even edit it (like writing a book), but if you settle for their words rather than your words, it isn't authentic. I used to send a lot of my written communications to my partner in school administration, Patsy Schwarm, and as I have mentioned before, she was someone who knew me, knew my personality, and knew my heart. She would sometimes say, "Great letter—but don't send it, it's too harsh, too emphatic, too emotional. If you still feel that way in the morning, write another one." Sometimes she would offer a different phrase or a different approach, but she never changed who I was, or made me less passionate about my job and life. Most of the time she was right, but her corrections blended with my style and message. They didn't change me. In addition to Pat, over a long career, I would give many of my writings to Sue, Dee, Nancy, or Marie, all trusted assistants who would look for the many spelling, grammar, or composition errors and fix them. At times they would say, "I don't get this paragraph," or "I don't think the parents will understand this statement." They didn't *change* me, they *corrected* me, or they *clarified* me. They knew that a statement, report, newsletter, letter, document, or any written information from the school, especially from the administration, would get a thousand times more criticism if the spelling or grammar were wrong. And when they corrected my content or choice of words they did it with tact or grace. They understood and applied the concept of kindness, of dipping the arrow in honey.

Know All Sides

Do your homework before you respond to any situation, write a conclusion, offer a verdict, or put anything in writing. Know all sides of the issue and speak fairly about it. Investigate every perspective you can think of, and when you feel you have covered all bases, ask another party whose intellect and temperament you respect—just to be sure.

Remember what we talked about in the first chapter, that you have the time to think before responding. You gain that time with a universally accepted statement, "I need to do a little homework before I respond," or "I really want to think and study this issue before I get back to you." Then remember that a time line is essential to retain trust. "I will contact you by the end of tomorrow." And even if you aren't done collecting all the needed information, you make the contact as promised with an update on your progress and a new date for the proposed conclusion.

I have said it before and it is worth repeating: don't rush your communications if research or study is warranted. Take the time to do it right. If people are anxious and don't think you need the time, carefully let them know that you do. You might say something like "This issue is important. It deserves some study to do it justice." If that doesn't sit well, so be it. A rash communication can sometimes do more damage than a one that is well thought-out. And again, I encourage careful proofreading of anything written or planned, and as often as possible, input from others who may see things from a slightly different, or totally different, viewpoint. For a guy like me who likes to get things done quickly and efficiently, this has been a discipline I have learned slowly and carefully over the years. Measure twice, cut once; write twice, publish once.

Communicate Efficiently

In a later chapter of this book you will find a long list of thoughts and ideas from many experts in education. One common element runs through that chapter: be efficient. Time management, tips for handling things in an organized manner, and ways to trim effort and time are the core of the commentary. Efficient communication is very important. When you talk, use your words carefully. Sometimes the less said is the safest, and often the most effective and appreciated. When you write a message follow a simple guideline: read and reduce. I do this all the time. One of my favorite teachers was Dean Buckingham.

(I talk about him throughout my book *Teachers Change Lives 24/7* because he had such a great impact on my life—and he literally caused me to become a speaker and author.)

Buckingham's encouragement was priceless. In his class we used a book called the *Elements of Style* by William Strunk. I still use this book today. One suggestion that Strunk gives is to construct clear, concise, and concrete sentences. That means to eliminate excessive verbiage and get to the point. This is not always easy, and sometimes authors may feel that it strips them of creativity. Not so. In fact it is still possible to be unique and to express your personality by being clear, concise, and to the point. How do you do this? Reread and simplify. If you think your statement is confusing, de-confuse it. If you think it takes too long to get the point across, rewrite and get there quicker. Reviewing all forms of communication often results in a more efficient product. Can you review a conversation? Certainly. If you are talking with someone and you are not sure if they understood the message, ask, "Does this make sense?" Or more concisely ask, "Make sense?" Often you will get a firm yes, sometimes a pause (meaning probably not) and sometimes a question.

Learn how to shorten your communications and how to use alternate forms of the communication processes to drive the point home. More as we progress...

Communication Is Visual

I'm not talking about smoke signals, although... Anyway, what you see affects what you think. When you communicate in person you add an element that affects your message. Think about it. When a speaker first comes on stage, even if they are talking, what do you do first? You size them up, check out their appearance, their posture, their dress, their grooming. You look from hair to shoes. You check for a watch, a wedding ring, jewelry, piercings, tattoos. You notice the oddities and irregularities. You check their smile, eyes, hand movements, and how or if they walk differently, or strut or slither. If their words don't interrupt your visual inspection, then you keep on looking. Hopefully the message will divert your eyes and make your brain focus on the words. Still, it's human nature to size up the presenter.

I'm not just talking about a stage presentation, I'm talking about an interview, a staff meeting, or when you walk into a classroom. I'm talking about you doing the very same thing when a parent walks into your office, or a teacher, or a salesperson. We first check out the visual before we focus on the auditory. Other things might creep into your immediate assessment, like a handshake, a smell, an aura of positivity, sadness, negativity, or blandness. You assess and you sense, and every step of this process is one ingredient added to the effectiveness, or lack of, in the communication process.

The good thing about this part of communication is that you have some control over it; in fact, you have a huge amount of control. Wearing a school shirt to a basketball game shows support. Wearing a school shirt to a funeral shows, well, it shows something. A firm handshake (male or female) shows confidence. Too firm or too weak show other attributes. Tattoos may cause a variety of responses, which should cause the tattooed to consider the consequences. Remember to know your audience. The same is true with hairstyle, clothing style, and other adornments. When in doubt, consider what the consequences might be.

A school administrator is a person held in high regard in most communities. Grandparents as well as students want the school administrator to be a good example of everything, from behavior to dress to language to action. So, it is imperative to remember that what you look like communicates a great deal in a short time. Looking like a professional can allow your communications to be focused on what you say rather than how you look. If others know you always look professional, they skip the "look-see" and focus on the message.

Communication Is Speaking

Speaking in public is the number one fear of Americans. It ranks higher than the fear of death! Of course administrators should have overcome this fear during their tenure as a teacher, assuming they went through the traditional route from the classroom to the principal's desk. However, teaching a class of third-graders, or a class of high school students, is usually not as intimidating as speaking before a room full of adults, and sometimes, angry adults, or speaking to a table full of school board members, or a group of professors considering approval of your thesis.

So, when the time comes for that prepared or impromptu question and answer session, consider these five ways to reduce your fear, from Dr. Preston Ni. (I have taken the liberty to use his headings, then I tweaked the explanations.)

1. Don't Expect Perfection from Yourself

No human is perfect, thus no speaker is perfect. As many times as I have taken the stage, I still stumble once in a while. When it is obvious, I make light of it. When it is not, I simply move on. If you expect perfection, you are in for real downer. Strive for acceptance and then always try to learn from the inevitable mistakes. Keep moving forward and do it with grace. Don't admit your mistakes, slide by them, unless they are so obvious, like falling over, and then laugh with the audience and keep going.

2. Avoid Equating Public Speaking to Your Self-Worth

"If you're reading this article, you're probably a successful professional who has worked hard to get to where you are today. Public speaking is only a small part of your overall professional ability. If you're not confident at it, there are many ways to help you improve. I've seen otherwise intelligent and capable professionals shrivel up on stage, as if suddenly nothing about them is right. Whether you're good at public speaking or not has nothing to do with your value as a person. It's simply a skill that you can learn and become better at with practice," says Dr. Ni.

There are books and articles and lots of help if you want to be a better public speaker. I have found the best way to improve is to ask someone you trust, "What worked, what could I do better, what should I not repeat?" Honest answers will help you improve. Make sure you are asking someone who will be objective, honest, and will offer constructive suggestions.

The School Principal's Toolbook

3. Avoid Being Nervous About Your Nervousness

If you aren't a bit nervous you aren't a bit human. Being concerned about being nervous adds another layer of anxiety. Accept the fact that you might sweat (wear a coat or white shirt), that you might have dry mouth (have a glass of water handy), that you might forget some words (highlight them on your script), that you might forget to look at all segments of the audience (write LOOK in the middle of each page), or you might lose track of where you are (check your notes to make sure they are in order and write the page numbers in BIG numbers, and check them once more right before you present). Be proactive and you reduce your anxiety. If you lose your place, quietly look for it and make the pause sound like it was planned. If your mouth goes suddenly dry, stop and take a sip of water when the audience is applauding. Learn the tricks and learn to accept the normal nervousness. Convert all of that into energy and passion!

4. Avoid Trying to Memorize Every Word

If you know your content and have read over the word-for-word script many times, then you do not need to memorize it. When I used to write out every word I would highlight key phrases and make sure I covered those pieces of specific information, then I filled in the in-between stuff. If I had studied my script well enough I had the confidence to scan the highlighted sections and know what to add. Then it just flowed. In fact, you may eventually just write out the key phrases and skip the word for word, making sure you stick to the topic and don't wander. If you try to memorize you have a much greater chance of error.

5. Avoid Reading Word for Word

Avoid reading your presentation word for word from a script. There's a big difference between reading and speaking. Plain reading is a way to disseminate information, often at the risk of audience comprehension. A speech that is read is quite often devoid of emotion and excitement. How many ways can you spell BORING?

The School Principal's Toolbook

When you speak you share emotions, movement, pauses, intonation, excitement, consideration, and, most of all, you share yourself.

6. They Want You to Succeed

I want to add a personal observation to Dr. Ni's list. The audience wants the speaker to succeed. This is important. When you give a presentation, address a crowd, or step behind the lectern, always remember that the audience is giving you an A. They don't want to be bored or disappointed. If you stumble, they are rooting for you. If you keep fumbling, are ill prepared, or read rather than talk, their patience will flounder. You have them from the start so all you need to do is keep them. They will give you space and be forgiving if you give your best. Remember that you start with an A. All you have to do is keep earning it.

Communication Is Attitude, Energy, and Honesty

You communicate mostly by being who you are. If you are a slug and meander through the halls with your head down, walk at half speed, and emit the brightness of a 15-watt bulb, you will unlikely find a wake of enthusiasm following you. If, however, you are a beacon of possibility, friendly and happy, encouraging and thoughtful, you may find hordes of excitement instead. List every teacher you know that has the personality of a wilted, sagging floral arrangement. I bet you can list a few. Now, list the educators you know who have influenced you, who had charisma and energy, who lit up every room they walked in. I bet you have a list. Why? Because we remember both ends of the spectrum.

So, if you are what you are, can you change who you are? Absolutely. The very fiber of your being is bendable and teachable. I have seen it happen and, as an administrator, I have helped it happen. Communicating what works, how it works, with an attitude that works. The very zest of your communications can drive the end result. If you have a passion for making a difference for kids, share it. If something moves you emotionally, be moved. If you don't like what you see, communicate it. If you appreciate and admire someone, tell them. If you see a staff member who simply looks great, with a new hairdo or an outfit that makes them look super, and you think it, then say it. It does no good in your memory bank, but multitudes of good if it is shared. "Joan, you look great today. You look like you are ready to change the world!" Who doesn't want to hear that? (Unless, of course, your name isn't Joan.)

As you work to improve your writing and speaking, try to improve your energy and attitude. Walk through the doors in the morning with an agenda of change, of support, of ideas, of goals. Stick to it with enthusiasm, and fight the battles as they come, with energy, always asking yourself, *"How can I make this challenge something that pushes us forward?"* Finish the day by asking (or writing), *"What did I do today that dented the universe?"*

Rejuvenation!

I have a few ideas for energy rejuvenation during the day. Take a hike when you need it. If you sense some negativity or lack of enthusiasm, get up and walk. I was fortunate in all my administrative positions to have an office within walking distance of a grade school. When I felt discouraged, or tired, or even unsure of what my next move was, I simply said to my trusty gatekeeper, I'm headed over to the primary building and I will be back in 20 minutes or less. That's all I said and then I walked over there, hoping someone was on recess and I would see them as I trekked to the building, or I would just go and walk the halls, visit a classroom, the gym, the art center, or even the office. I would "see" why we are in this business. Kids would eagerly come up and say hello. I could jump rope, or throw a ball, or grab a paintbrush and add a stroke to a kid's artwork, or I could walk through a room with hands waving in the air, with teachers eager to say "Hi!" Kids would do the same, and that always made the trip worthwhile. Or I could go to the office and shake the hands of a parent or a visitor, or a combination of any of the above. It would lift my temporary discouragement, and I'd go back revitalized.

When I was excessively tired from a long board meeting, supervising a late game or concert, or maybe working late, or it was just one of those days when my high level of energy wore me out, I would say to my administrative assistant, "I need 15 minutes." That was code for *I'm going to close the door, turn off the lights, lie down on the floor, turn on my CD player, and sleep for 10 minutes*. Yep, a midday nap! I would do that about five times a year, when I was just running on less than empty. The code also meant that if my door doesn't open in 15 minutes, give me a call. That never happened. I conked out for about 10 minutes, woke up, opened the door, and went back to work a new man. You see, unlike the teachers, I didn't have a prep period, a regulated lunch hour, or even starting and ending times. The administrator usually runs on full speed from early to late, forfeiting a regular schedule to accommodate the needs of the kids, staff, and district. So my 15 minutes of solitude were well earned, and in truth, they gave the district, at no charge, a refreshed and ready-to-go me for the rest of the day. It was one way to keep communicating through my attitude and revitalized energy.

Trust

I was told, and have repeated thousands of times, two mantras for educators, especially administrators, who want to be effective and respected:

(1) Never, never, never lie, and
(2) Never, never, never gossip.

If you want to reduce or eliminate any chance of being respected, or any chance that the troops will trust, believe, or follow you, then be dishonest or gossip. Both are career killers. Your ability to effectively communicate in any fashion will be dampened if people cannot trust you. Your ability to change or motivate the staff in a positive direction will fall off the cliff if they can't trust you. Dishonesty and gossip stop progress and can actually reverse it.

One of the best teachers I ever worked with, named Carol, could turn gossip around in a heartbeat. If the staff was talking about a student and it morphed into gossip about the parents—their lifestyle, their habits, and so on—she would quietly reverse the conversation by saying something like, "We really don't know anything about what goes on in their home, but we sure do know the needs of Otto. What can we do to provide him with... (fill in the blanks)?" Wham, gossip turned into a professional goal.

I was sitting in the teacher's room one day when this very thing happened about a fifth-grade boy named Willie, who I had in my physical education class. The talk was about Willie's dysfunctional parents and was based on silly rumors that did nothing but make fun of them. Carol said that Willie came to school with so many needs, and basic hygiene was one of them. She had shared this with the counselor and hopefully help was being made available to the family, but Willie still came with un-brushed teeth and wearing dirty clothes. Because of that conversation we had a change in the physical education class curriculum for a day and I went over how to brush your teeth, how to shampoo your hair, how to shower, etc. The boys thought it was great and I even had some soap, shampoo, and a few new toothbrushes available for those who might need them. Willie took the supplies and learned from the lesson. It was a win-win-win for everyone, thanks to Carol converting gossip into good.

As an administrator, always check your honesty and gossip level. Be known as the person who everyone can count on and who will turn negativity into productivity through communications that are honest, sincere, and energized.

Communicating with Zoom

"Zoom Learning" is the way kids learn today. See the next chapter on "Zoom Learning" and the implications it has for educators, especially administrators.

One very important component of "Zoom Learning" is communications. In fact communications have changed almost everything about education in just a few quick years. Think about it. The iPad was released on April 3, 2010, and it started a revolution in communication. It hasn't been many years since the handheld phone went from a boxy contraption that had an antenna and a lunchbox device for its storage and battery to what it is today. Now almost everyone has a cell phone. (According to statistics as recently as 2013, there are almost as many cell phone numbers in the world as there are people on the planet—that happened in about 20 years!) Of course, cell phones aren't just phones, they send voice calls, text calls, and even photos. Many send email, connect to the Internet, take great pictures and videos, and are the source of a number of ways to communicate that weren't invented just a few years ago—some were invented last week or in the time it takes you to read this chapter.

Social media and networking have a short history. In 2001, Fotolog, Sky Blog, and Friendster appeared. In 2003, MySpace, LinkedIn, Last.fm, Tribe.net, and Hi5 came on the scene. Then, in 2004, names like Facebook Harvard, Dogster, and Mixi evolved. During 2005 it was Yahoo! 360, YouTube, Cyworld, and BlackPlanet. From the early days to the present, many companies have emerged and many have disappeared. As I'm writing this book the most popular social networks are Facebook, Twitter, LinkedIn, Pinterest, Google+, Tumblr, Instagram, VK, Flickr, Myspace, Meetup, Tagged, Ask.fm, MeetMe, and Classmates. (Honestly, I haven't heard of several of these, but millions of you have.) In fact, the last on the list (Classmates) has 15 million users, while the first (Facebook) has 900 million. And this list doesn't even come close to naming the new sites that are gaining popularity while some of the top hitters are fading. And I haven't even mentioned social game sites or video gaming in general.

Schools across the country are beginning to teach social media, especially how to use Facebook and Twitter. Angel Fuentes, an assemblyman from New Jersey, was recently quoted as saying, "Kids should never be held back later in life because of their social media use today. It is our job to prepare students for the professional world, one that increasingly takes place online." He proposed a bill that will require students in grades 6-8 to take a class that will teach the appropriate use of various social media sites. The course also includes study of cyber bullying, cyber safety, and ethics. We didn't have classes like this a few short years ago because we didn't have cyber—anything!

As an administrator today if you aren't in tune with the way kids communicate then you aren't doing a very good job. Harsh? Maybe, but true. Kids and parents communicate through texting and social media. I have many grandkids and I communicate with each differently. One even calls me on the phone! They message me, Instagram me, Facebook me, email me, and one sends me to sites I never heard of—until he introduces them to me. That's not only fun, it's a great way to stay in touch. That is how today's generation communicates. And who knows how newborns will communicate in just a few years. One thing is certain, if I don't stay in tune with how my students communicate now, I will be lost, uninformed, and out of the loop...

I even have a teenage niece who started to share her thoughts about makeup and social issues on a homemade YouTube account when she was a tween. She is still in high school, has about 250,000 followers, earned $20,000 doing this last year, just signed a contract with a major manufacturer, and will probably have a career from her interest and appropriate use of social media. She advocates doing things right and is a great role model. Kids know about Zoom. You should too.

This is not a book intended to go into detail, but to be a "toolbook" that you can use to expand your leadership skills and thinking. Ronald Williamson and Howard Johnston have written a great book entitled *The School Leader's Guide to Social Media*. It is an extremely informative read for administrators and all educators. In the book they discuss ways to embrace social media as an educational tool—and as reality.

Williamson and Johnston begin their argument for social media by providing school leaders with this list of top 10 reasons they should focus on social media:

1. It's here to stay and it's only getting bigger.
2. Kids are using it to talk about you and your school.
3. It's the way kids communicate.

4. It's a new workplace and higher education communication standard.
5. Mobile devices put a computer in nearly everyone's hands.
6. It has huge potential for school leadership.
7. It's a great way to engage kids in instruction.
8. Communication is instantaneous and widespread.
9. It's beyond the control of the school, but it can be used well in school.
10. Schools can model and help kids learn responsible use of social media.

It's time we engage in the new way to communicate. It's time we used, understood, and taught social media. Consume it or be eaten by it. It's our choice.

Warnings

Do you have clear and understandable policies in place dealing with cell phone use in the schools, at school events, or on school property? Do you have rules in place for the use of phone cameras, sexting, cyberbullying, illegal transactions, or cheating? Are your policies understood by your students, parents, community, staff, police, and the board? The best policies are those that were developed jointly by all of these groups.

Do you have school or district communication systems for posting homework, messages, talking with parents, sending alerts, or for other uses? Has each staff member (including you) been completely trained? Have you trained your students' parents and the community in general on their use? Do you know what the recipients expect from communications sent by the school? Have you ever surveyed or asked them?

Have you talked to your staff about their role with social media, the dangers of "friending" students, and the proper use of the district-wide communication network?

Have you conducted even the most basic training with staff on the correct way to send emails and/or texts, what not to say, how to check for copies being sent, how to reread even the most basic message? Do the users know how to find out exactly who is receiving the message, what it says, and if it makes sense? Have you warned them about sending a response during the wrong time of the day or night?

There are so many things to consider that a basic Communications 101 on social media, texting, emails, sending photos, talking to parents, setting parameters, and much more is a good idea to be conducted often with all of your team members.

And, finally, do you bring every new employee, even substitutes, up to speed on the rules and policies about using the school or district communication network? A short YouTube video made for this very purpose is something that helps parents and staff members alike.

Writing

The old standby form of communication is the written word. It is also a very important part of social networking, but it seems that "u can get by w/ shrtcts" in today's writing styles. Just beware that not everybody understands symbols or abbreviations, nor does everybody appreciate them. Certainly when you write something in the form of a newsletter or document, even a greeting card or formal letter, you need to be able to express yourself fully and well.

Here are a few rules and reminders worth noting:

1. If your handwriting is poor, type or print.
2. Use spell checker and grammar check.
3. Even after the computer checks your writing, reread it.
4. Proof everything. Proof it twice if it's going to be printed.
5. If it is going to be printed, *have someone read it for understanding*, then proof it, then proof it again. Get the idea?
6. People will read the first and last paragraphs of longer letters or reports. Make the middle count as well. Connect everything.
7. The envelope is important too. Make it look professional.
8. Finally, and most important of all: proofread everything. Is it important? The books I write are proofread several times, by professional editors and readers, and we still find errors.

9. Write, read, cut excessive words or phrases, read again, have someone else read for clarity, proof it again, print it out, read it again, then distribute it.
10. Oh yes—did I mention this?—proofread everything.

Communication vs. Information

If I send you a letter, or a newsletter, or write an article, that is "information." If I send you a notice about when paychecks will be distributed, that is a "dictate." If I tell you about a change in the schedule that I want you to know and share, and I need to hear from you, then I am communicating with you. I'm not nitpicking here. *Communication* is not complete until it is two-way.

"How are you?" is a question awaiting an answer. The answer closes and completes the communication. If I wish you happy birthday in a Facebook comment or in a greeting card, I'm not asking for a response, I am sending a message. If I ask how you are feeling, I am asking for a response and the communication is open until you close it.

When I sent messages to my staff and wanted a response I would put RSVP at the end. That meant "send me a response."

"Got it" was usually an adequate answer. "Thanks for the information" worked. When I received the response the communication was closed and I knew they had received something that I thought was important enough to ask for acknowledgment. Too often we send "information" in place of "communication" and the connection is lost.

"How did the new curriculum go this morning?" in a text asks for a response. If you get a communication that begs an answer, provide it. If you need an answer, ask for it. Two-way communication solves a lot of problems and clarifies a lot of issues.

20 Slides/20 Seconds

There is a process that is gaining popularity in education right now. It has a formal, trademarked name that is worth examining: Pecha Kucha. I encourage you to learn about this process and the "brand." It represents the idea I simply call "20 Slides/20 Seconds." This method of communication is based on either a PowerPoint or Keynote (or other form) of slide presentation programming. The format is simple. You make your presentation fit on 20 slides, and each slide changes automatically every 20 seconds. I have found this idea to be of great help in getting people to learn about presentation rules and methods. The presentation is usually accompanied with a verbal script, either taped or given live, that follows the 20/20 format. I have used this method many times in developing a concise, short, to-the-point, easy-to-follow presentation on a specific topic. It is a great way for kids to write reports, groups to create productions, or teachers to share with other teachers. No one gets bored since there is hardly enough time for boredom to take hold. It forces the presenter to fill the time portals precisely and with intelligible content. It is not a new idea, but it is relatively new to education. I strongly encourage your review of this process.

Faculty Meetings, Newsletters, Website

Each of these topics—faculty meetings, newsletters, websites—could be fodder for another book. In truth, they are! There are several books about how to run productive meetings, create effective newsletters, and develop websites. There are also many academies or workshops on procedures and technology that help with all three. I encourage you to study these topics and if you are fortunate to have talented folks who can help with the writing, coordination, and planning of these three forms of communication, recognize their importance and use them appropriately. Let's talk briefly about each topic.

Faculty Meetings
First, the faculty meeting is when you bring together your team for an important sharing process. It should be something they look forward to, not hate. It should respect your time and energy—and theirs. It should be a time of growth, not just discipline. It should be a time of positivity, not doom. It should not be filled with administrivia, things that could be on a "con-

sent agenda" and discussed only if needing clarification. It should be a time that has a set and firm beginning and a set ending. It should be mandatory for everyone, with understood exceptions. "Joe is not here today because he is coaching a baseball game." It should have structure and a time for discussion. You shouldn't open or close a meeting with bad news. If you have to share something you don't support (like a new curricular mandate), remember that your energy and expectation and attitude will set the tone from that moment on. If you want to serve food, have it ready before the meeting starts and make it clear that they will get to business at 3:40 exactly— please get your pizza or apple (I want the pizza) first. Include something in the meeting on a regular basis that says thank you.

Newsletters

Your building newsletter needs to coordinate with district newsletters. You should never, ever upset the district newsletter process. Make your newsletters interesting, relevant, and have a reason for existing. If they include necessary schedules for events, buses, or parent meetings, make sure everyone knows that. Have a distribution process that works. I suggest that all newsletters that are hard copied also be included on the district website for full accessibility at any time. Write well, follow good communication procedures, and make the newsletter a valuable and enjoyable asset.

Websites

Your website is the number one way people check out the value of your school system. It's number one in visual communicative importance—by a landslide. It's also the most often used tool to research where a family with kids wants to live.

The importance of a clear, catchy, confident, competent, concise, "pretty," well-designed, information-loaded, easy-to-navigate, and up-to-date website is almost immeasurable. Do you think I am going overboard here? *I'm not.* Look at your district's website. See how easy it is to get to your school's location. Can the reader *easily* find your name, your contact information, the school's location, address, phone number, even directions? Can the reader discover quickly what you are most proud of or where your school excels? Is it evident that you know what you are doing? Have you ever asked anyone who doesn't know your school to visit the website and report back its high points or faults? If the answer is no, then right now write a note on a piece of paper (or in your phone) to do this.

Did you write that note? Don't underestimate the importance of your website.

Is the information on your website *current* and interesting? Does it make you want to visit? If you don't give every question I have asked an A, then you need to work on the website. Check every section, too, not just your school's part. It's just like a barrel of bananas, one bad one ruins the barrel. All right, I know that bananas don't come in barrels, but you got the point, right?

Summary

How do you summarize something that is so complicated and involved as communication when it really is a fundamental part of everything we do in education? You can't. You just have to remember that who you are and what you stand for is reflected in how you communicate. Equally important is how you expect others to communicate. This part of education should never be just taken for granted. You set the standard, and that standard for your school is judged by how it is written and looks.

I once saw on a school billboard (which is kind of like a website on poles), "We edducate!" It made me laugh for about five miles, but I suspect that wasn't its intent.

Chapter 8

Zoom Learning:
Understanding and Embracing How Kids Learn

There is no one word or term for "the way kids learn today," so I invented one. I call it "Zoom Learning." It may be one of the most important concepts in this book if we are truly interested in capturing the minds and enthusiasm of today's student. How did the term come to be?

The dictionary tells us that zoom means "increasing the focus, when using a special lens on a camera, or moving at a rapid rate of speed." Then it lists scores of synonyms for zoom, like bolt, bucket, bustle, dart, dash, flash, fleet, flit, fly, haste, hasten, hurry, hustle, race, rocket, run, rush, sail, scoot, shoot, speed, sprint, trot, whirl, whisk, wing, and zip.

And "learning" is what we do and help make possible for kids 24/7.

But "zoom" has a deeper meaning too.

Let me explain. Years ago there was a classic TV commercial for the Mazda Miata. It took place on the Gothard Pass in the Swiss Alps, which is a world-famous, often-photographed winding road in the mountains. In that commercial as a sleek, fast, delicious-looking sports car winds its way down the mountain, a cute little boy appears from behind a rock just as the car whizzes by. The kid turns from the car, looks into the camera, and says, "Zoom, zoom!"

That advertisement has stuck in my mind forever, probably because I could have been that boy. I was always amazed by cars, and still am! It captured the wonder of the car in the eyes of a little boy—the speed, the rush, the breathtaking exhilaration. Million of others still remember that boy's wide-eyed awe too, and his "zoom-zoom" whisper.

Move forward a few years to a trip my wife and I took with five of our grandkids, then 9-16, from our home near St. Louis to a Midwestern activity mecca called Branson, Missouri. What

The School Principal's Toolbook

was so life-changing about a five-hour drive? It opened my eyes to the real meaning of the word "zoom," and each of the seven of us in the SUV played a part.

Barb, my wife, is very intelligent but she is geographically challenged. So she has mastered GPS. She loves it. When she said, "Let me drive to Branson while you sit with the boys," that was better than a fair trade to a guy who logs a ton of miles on a regular basis. So, Barb and her buddy, the GPS, were in control.

Sitting next to her, the oldest of the grandkids, at 16, was armed with a smartphone. Probably an iPhone, but honestly I don't remember. What I do remember is that she was using it all the time, not just to communicate or take pictures, but also to *answer her own questions.* When we traveled near Lebanon, Missouri, I remember her asking if Lebanon was the name of a country and then, before you could answer, she said "Never mind. I found it!" A bit later she asked if we knew about Route 66, and then proceeded to give us its history. She then asked if we had ever heard of a TV show in the '60s named *Route 66.* Then, had we ever heard of Kookie Byrnes? She was a perpetual encyclopedia of information during the entire trip. By the way, this granddaughter was not an A student, though she has A abilities. She was never inspired by her teachers to reach her potential. Homework was not her favorite thing, and academics took a back seat to anything spelled "SOCIAL." Yet there she was, doing educational research, investigating one thing that was connected to another, infatuated with learning, not because she had to but because she could.

Sitting in the middle seats were two more of the grandkids, both nine-year-old girls, cousins, and best friends. They had conjured up some contraption that connected two sets of earbuds to one handheld device, probably an iPod Touch or something that sounds like that. They were literally dancing in their seats to a Michael Jackson video. Later they connected to a word game, and then they even played a digital version of the old license plate game. They were actively engaged, having a ball, and learning along the way. They are bright kids. They played math games, spelling games, drawing games, and even did some interesting moves to music for most of the trip.

The School Principal's Toolbook

The back seat was testosterone alley. It was occupied with three males and three devices. I was in one corner with an iPad. I was working on an article, writing about technology. Next to me were my two oldest grandsons. (We left the baby grandson home with his parents!) The two 12-year-olds sitting with me are also cousins and best friends. One had a DS, the other a DSI. These are handheld video game devices with the ability to create media. One device was more expensive, and more capable, than the other. After a while the oldest boy, sitting next to me, asked if I knew what they were doing. I feigned an answer that had something to do with battling each other on some solar planet shooting Frisbee-like ammunition at spaceships while trying to earn points or ammo, or something, and thus becoming the disc-throwing champions of the solar system. Andrew gave me that shoulder shrug that said, "What are we going to do with Gramps?" Then he said, no, they weren't playing games. They had made something. And there before my eyes was a photo of me using the iPad. He pushed a button and the photo morphed into iPadMan, Super Hero of the Universe. I watched an amazing and creative movie clip unfold before my eyes. It was complete with script, music, and a story line. They had produced this with their devices, fingers, and brains.

After the initial 15 or 20 minutes of laughing and talking about what was ahead in Branson for the next three days, everyone plugged in and began the trip, all engaged, all happy. Barb was plugged into GPS, and the rest of us were using some device that either had us connected to the world via the Internet, to games that educated, or to applications that allowed creativity, or in my case, work. We were all learning, doing research, writing, drawing, singing, or dancing. That's when it hit me. As the car was speeding along Route 44, we were moving just as fast through technology, zipping through digital opportunities, and having a great time stretching our brains. That's when that look on that little boy's face when that Miata whipped by flashed into mind—and out came the word "zoom"—how we learn today. A new definition for a word that typically means speed or to bring to focus, both still applicable.

Thus, for me, the story of "Zoom Learning" began.

What Does This Mean to Principals?

Zoom Learning (the way we learn today) may be one of the most important ideas explained in this book. I fully believe that the concept, when fully implemented, will drastically improve the learning atmosphere in schools. Some principals have a grasp on it already, while many struggle with its implementation. The idea is simple—teach the way kids learn best. Why change things? Because kids today don't learn the way most of their teachers did.

Think about it. Most of us used pencil, paper, books, and chalkboards. Even the old process of introducing the topic, teaching the topic, providing for guided practice on the topic, and then testing the topic has changed. A new teaching style called "flipped classrooms" transposes the entire process from school to home and home to school—more on this later.

Kids today don't go out to play as much as we used to, if at all. Outside play may be limited to organized sports or arranged playdates with families and friends. Leaving in the morning and coming home before the streetlights come on during the summer has been replaced with video gaming or social networking. Kids today do more screen time than just about any other activity. TV, tablets, and computer games are huge consumers of time. A recent survey indicated that of the 95% of kids between 12 and 17 who go online daily, 62% go to a social network, 43% update or check friends' status, 36% send an instant message, 34% listen to downloaded music, 32% send an email, and 15% do schoolwork (*District Administrator*, 6/14). These statistics change all the time as more and more kids use a greater variety of "tools" and the Internet becomes more widely available. Kids are making friends on the screen rather than at the park.

Ask students a question, and if they have access to the web they can process an answer almost before you are done asking the question. Far-fetched? Not at all. I recently heard a teacher tell this story, "I don't have the kids memorize the capitals of the states anymore. Instead, I ask them to research the capitals. Then they actively discuss the capitals, can 'see' them, they remember them far better, and they know a lot more information." She continued by saying that in class she will give a pair of students the name of a state. She gives them 15 minutes to gather information on the capital and what makes the state interesting. They are preparing to give a two-minute report about their state. In 15 minutes the kids are ready to go! They share videos and photos of the capital, as well as how to spell its name. These are fourth-graders and the reports she shared were amazing. In a couple of days they covered all of the states with a variety of media, technology, and interesting facts—and she did almost zero teaching, beyond a lot of encouraging and directing. In fact, she said that every time they do this, she learns more. She also asked the kids to come up with clues to remember the names. One student said he thinks of Abraham Lincoln hopping around a farmer's field with big springs on his feet to remember that *Springfield* is the capital of Illinois. And here is the big bonus—kids *like* this project, they *learn* from the activity, and they *remember* what they learned. *This is Zoom Learning.*

Another item she shared: She tries to pair up students who have different technology backgrounds or opportunities so that one can learn new techniques from the other as they do the research. She also said that very quickly they learn to use PowerPoint or Keynote presentations for their reports.

I also know a principal who has incorporated the term "Zoom Learning" in his regular instructional leadership vocabulary, and has teachers share the ways kids are using it regularly. The teachers then share the new teaching methods they learn with each other. They have a Zoom Learning network that each teacher gets as an email. I have suggested they have a Zoom Learning 20 slides/20 seconds presentation at each faculty meeting. (20 slides/20 seconds is covered in the chapter on communications.)

Zoom Samples

WARNING! As soon as I write anything about specifics of technology I date the book. We all know that many aspects of technology are obsolete by the time they hit print. The same is true with Zoom Learning. So let me share what's happening as

I write this book. What we do today may very well be replaced by what we do next week. If you are reading this a year after its first publication you're likely to say, *"Really? That's old stuff, Burgett!"*

South Korea Winds Up, Then Balks

The South Korean government, in 2011, said that all students would be paper-bookless by 2015. All books would be digitalized and all students would have devices. This set a standard that induced our own government to set a goal that every student would have an e-reader by 2017. That sounds reasonable. Except that the South Korean government, one of the world's leaders in education, balked. They revisited their goals and decided that maybe books (printed on paper) had a place, and that younger students shouldn't rely entirely on devices. Even the experts on the subject battle what is right and what is best when it comes to technology in the schools. Maybe they will balk again and reverse their reversal!

The Backpack

One valid trend will be replacing the traditional backpack with a tablet, or some newer type of device. Why do I think so? My current tablet allows me to carry hundreds of books, many dictionaries, word source documents, a scientific calculator, a mapping program that beats both navigation systems in two of my cars, a level (yes, the kind you use for hanging pictures), a fine camera that takes photos and videos, a program for creating and sharing slide presentations (PowerPoint, Keynote, and more), a link to the Internet (which means I can find almost anything almost anywhere), and about 200 powerful apps. Did I mention that it also stores hundreds (in my case, thousands) of photos and songs?

What can these apps (meaning applications) do?

* Some of the apps can focus (using the camera) on a sign written in another language, then project that on my screen so it reads in English, or visa versa.

* One app, when opened, shows all the stars, planets, even spacecraft in the sky, and is linked to GPS, so when I move around, the view on my screen shows me exactly what I should be seeing when I look up into the sky.
* Another app allows me to talk to my tablet which then does what I tell it to do, such as write and send a text, an email, a letter, a note—or open an application, find an address, check my calendar, even get me data.
* I just "asked" an app who will be pitching for the Cubs in tonight's baseball game. My tablet said, "For the Cubs it's Jake Arrieta, for the Braves, Alex Wood."
* In the last hour I pushed a button on my tablet and asked if was going to rain this afternoon, what I had on my calendar for tomorrow, and when a certain new car was going to hit the showroom. All three questions were answered promptly and correctly. I pushed one button for each and talked to my tablet like it was a personal servant. It is.

Will a tablet-like device replace a backpack of paper, books, writing tools, and research documents? It should and it will; for me it has. And since my cell phone is synced to my tablet, it does everything the tablet does, but with a smaller screen and keyboard. What will the next-generation tablet look like and do? It may come in a variety of shapes and sizes, and in all probability it may be provided by the family rather than the school. It may be a normal part of communication, safety, and existence. It will be less expensive, it will do more, and it will do it easier. It will likely replace writing with dictating. It will know its owner in ways we cannot comprehend today. It may also open my checking account by retina identity. It may also tell me where you are and with whom. Imagine, too, if we had a way to know where our kids were every minute of every day, and be able to keep them safe.

This is not my father's world, it's a zoom world, and in only a matter of years most students at most levels (kindergarten to calculus and beyond) will carry almost every tool they need in a compact electronic device. Part of that device may even be somehow connected to our body.

With thousands of apps being created every week, and the number of apps available in 2014 already in the millions, the number of opportunities for finding an app that will assist learners and teachers is almost limitless.

I remember way back to my teaching years, just before man took his first step in space, how limited I was in finding resources that dealt with topics like photosynthesis. I had the textbook, the encyclopedia, and if I journeyed to the library, I might be able to dig up some college texts and articles, but then I had to write the information down or wait for Xerox to invent the copier before I could share anything with my students. Now I just hit the talk button on my tablet and ask it for "apps dealing with photosynthesis." In a second I literally have a list of dozens. I can then ask for YouTube videos on photosynthesis, and again dozens will appear. Going deeper, I can then ask my tablet to go to Ted.com and find lectures on photosynthesis—poof, another long list will magically appear. While I am at it, I can ask for "photosynthesis teaching lessons" and I will be directed to plans for just about every grade level.

This is how kids do their research, how Zoom Learning works, and how teachers need to think. "This is not my father's Oldsmobile" was a tagline a few years ago when Oldsmobile introduced a new, sportier model. But times change; today they don't even make Oldsmobiles anymore. Today's learning, Zoom Learning, is not the same as my father's learning, or my learning, or most of the learning that today's teachers had in their "good old school days." No, Zoom Learning is a hybrid that runs on electricity or gas or maybe hydrogen. Its fun, it's here, it's what you need to push every day with every member of the team.

Google vs. Apple

The big players today may still be the big players in a few years. Google has gone from typing something in a bar on your browser, and seeing what comes up, to things like Google Apps, Google Hangouts, Google Art Project, Google Docs and a myriad of other options, most of them "Googliscious." Apple changes its products at least two times a year, and soon, more frequently. Yesterday's phone is today's handheld, super impressive, multi-tasking, mini-computer. The tablet is a thin, all-inclusive device that went from game playing to providing almost every feature a laptop can do—and *more*. It is a learning lab, a powerful computer, and a library that fits in a purse or tucked under your arm. It seeks connection, finds it, and the rest is up to you. Are these the only players in town? Not by a long shot, but basically today these powerhouses call those shots. Their research and educational departments set the stage for newer technology and the incentive for increasing the numbers of apps. It is worth your while to know these technology giants, get hooked to their new products, and follow their developments.

Knowing the History

It isn't hard to figure out how we got to Zoom. It started when someone took an old typewriter and stuck an electric motor inside it. They figured out that we could produce more products, more quickly, and with fewer tangled typing bars if we turned the old manual typewriters into a machine that processed one letter at a time, synced to hitting one key at a time. (I know that some of you younger readers may not have any idea of what I am talking about, but stick with me). The electric typewriter kicked off Zoom Learning in a strange, slow, kind of weird way. My graduation gift from high school was an electric typewriter and I thought I had fallen in front of the cutting edge. But what did it do for education? Not much really. It allowed us to type faster. It might have been the "Z," the first letter, in Zoom Teaching.

Then came computers. First big ones, room-sized, then smaller ones but still industrial-sized. Then computers you could actually buy and use at home. Commodore Pets, the Apple I, and other little machines that had tiny capacities and no apps as we know them today. Schools started to catch on with computers in the mid '80s. The Internet was introduced later. It came to life in the early '90s, but didn't reach schools until the mid '90s. Was education really transformed by the computer? Not yet. Curriculum-related data was difficult to find;

the computer was used more for production of reports, data collection, organization, and manipulation. Only when the World Wide Web became popular and was populated with information did the computer serve as a station to collect information. Guidance counselors were the first to use it on a large scale, collecting information about jobs and higher education.

The first tablet was an iPad. Since 2010 tablets have ruled. Now, millions of different kinds of tablets are sold each month. Who do you know in education that doesn't have some form of tablet? And with tablets came the most transforming educational product ever, the app. The definition of an app is a self-contained program or piece of software designed to fulfill a particular purpose. As I said, it's an application, especially as downloaded by a user to a mobile device. Apps, videos, digital lessons, websites, the Internet, all have all changed the face of education. So finally we have reached "Zoom Learning"!

I suspect that some day I won't be typing a chapter for a book on my laptop or tablet, I will be thinking it and the words will be captured and printed before my very eyes. Just like the app on my iPad that found the definition for the word app when I asked, "What is the definition of app?" I will someday just think the question and the answer will manifest itself in words, probably in the air where I can see them, hear them, even feel them. And to get to this state of technology I will probably receive instructions from one of my grandkids, again!

So How Do We Learn to Zoom?

A few years ago I gave a keynote presentation opening a rather large school district. This was a day or two before the kids arrived and school went into high gear. The superintendent, as often happens, preceded my presentation. He gave a welcoming address. During the address he forgot the name of one of his veteran principals and then spent a great deal of time on administrivia. So far, it was a disaster. This is a meeting that should have been encouraging and motivating. It never got any better. But at the end of his talk he announced that over the past week every fifth-grade classroom had a "smart board" installed on the wall with a ceiling-mounted projector. I didn't think much of it until I noticed that no one in the audience seemed excited. In fact, I could hear audible moaning. "That's odd," I thought to myself and turned to the assistant superintendent who had hired me and whispered out loud, "They don't seem too excited."

"They aren't," he said. "They didn't know they were being ordered and they have had no training in using smart boards. They are the first ones in the district to get them," he told me. I was shocked. The brand of smart boards they received were top of the line and this purchase had to be very expensive. The superintendent didn't give any expectations, announce any training, nor did he offer any encouragement about what teachers could do with this new technology. He simply announced their arrival and availability and moved on to something else that I quickly forgot.

Is this an extreme example? *I hope so.* Because in today's economic climate a surprise mass purchase of expensive technology is not the norm. And it should be an exciting announcement followed by the assurance that training would be provided; even better, a live demonstration right there to get listeners excited about the limitless opportunities a full-blown, connected-to-the-Internet smart board can bring. None of this happened, and no training was purchased or on the horizon.

In education we often put our dollars into things rather than training—not the best order of expenditures. And we often buy things before we build ownership, which again is not a bright practice.

When I was done speaking, I received a warm ovation that I much appreciated. That told me they needed this type of presentation, one that was helpful and encouraging. I also talked about the need to teach the way kids learn, with viable examples of how to make this happen. When I was preparing to leave several teachers came up and almost circled me. I soon discovered that most of them were fifth-grade teachers. All were asking the same thing. "What do we do with these smart boards?" Many were veteran teachers who had zero experience with technology. They were standing in mass seeking my help.

The School Principal's Toolbook

I gathered my thoughts and came up with what I thought, at the time, was not only a politically correct but also helpful list of possible answers. Here is what I said in almost exactly the same terminology.

1. Check with the technology department in your district to see if formal training has been scheduled, either by the manufacturer or another professional development provider. If it hasn't, ask for it and get a time line.
2. Introduce the equipment to the kids on the first day and tell them you plan to use it soon, and that you are excited about it. Tell them it is brand-new and you are anxious to learn all that it can do in the classroom.
3. As your students (fifth-graders) if there are any "gamers" who would like to tackle a special project. (Gamers are kids proficient with video games and/or computers.) Try to assemble a group of four to six kids, boys and girls, and call them a "special commission."
4. Have this "special commission" meet with you and give them the instruction manual for the smart board (make a copy first!) and ask them to do two things: set up the equipment per the instructions and prepare a brief tutorial for you and possibly the class. Give them three or four days and let them meet during lunch, etc. Encourage other teachers to do the same thing.
5. Ask the staff if anyone has experience on the smart board who can give you some directions.
6. Once the kids get involved in your class, and other classes, compare notes. There maybe a kid genius in the group that everyone can learn from. Now, learn from the kids!
7. See what happens, and I am guessing you will all be surprised and happy.
8. And while doing all of this, remain positive and don't share your initial disappointment.

Think this wouldn't work? Wrong! It worked fine and within a week or two most of those teachers were off and running with the white boards. Better yet, each teacher had a cadre of middle-sized experts helping them along the way. It was win-win for everyone. Actually win-win-win, with students, teachers, and learning.

Google It

Another approach, and the way I learned to put together some really terrific professional presentations, is simply to "Google it." I just type my question in the Google.com bar and usually within seconds I am pointed the right direction. I remember the first time I created a movie on the laptop. I knew zero about how to do it. I "Googled" every step, beginning with, "How do I make an instruction movie?" Through research, trial and error, and a few chats with experts I never met and will never know, plus a pinch of blind courage, I ventured into the world of cyberspace and learned a ton. I still "Google" it many times a day! In fact, this morning in the high school Sunday school class I teach we twice discussed topics that needed some research. Chandler, one of my 13-year-old boys, opened his PDA (personal digital assistant), probably an iPhone, and in a matter of seconds had used a map app to locate a city, a street, and a specific answer to our question. A few minutes later Siri was used to find the number of worldwide members of a specific religion. Kids have no fear when it comes to technology and can often direct a teacher to the best apps or resources.

Assign It

Remember the example about teaching photosynthesis? A very creative but technologically challenged veteran teacher participated in a discussion I was holding about technology in the classroom. I used the photosynthesis example and she took it to a different level. She told her students that the next unit (after the one they were just beginning) would be on a certain subject, and she wrote the subject on the board, or screen, or smart board. She said she was offering some extra-credit points for anyone who could find some information on the web that would be helpful and interesting in presenting this subject matter. They had a week to give her both the location and a paragraph of why this was interesting. If she used their suggestion they would get so many points, and if she didn't use it, but it was worthy, they would also receive so many points. She had already directed her students to YouTube, the Kahn Academy, Ted.com, TedEd.com, and other possible sites for mini lectures, movies, presentations, etc. Each is a different resource. She also said that just a Google search would be helpful. She added this caveat: the first person with a specific site is the only one who gets credit for that site.

In one day she had ample materials to supplement the curriculum, and most of it was worthy of her consideration. Kids received extra credit for doing the research, the lesson was enhanced with meaningful information, and everyone benefited as a result. Win-win-win. The student, the teacher, and the class are all were winners in the process.

Resource It

When I was working with a district in Alaska I was very impressed with their use of the Internet and how they involved the kids with smart boards and tablets, but I was surprised that they still didn't allow kids to carry their phone (or PDA) with them during the day. We talked about their robust use of technology and how they might incorporate cell phones as part of the curriculum. I suggested they research "*smartbrief.com*" and then select the educational issues, especially the NBPTS (National Board of Professional Teaching Standards) issues, and search for cell phone use in the classrooms. In seconds they had loads of related articles from schools and organizations with hands-on, expert experience. They were amazed, and things in that district changed quickly.

SmartBrief is a series of email newsletters for professionals that cover various topics with a variety of focus. Under "education" you can find classroom, educational leadership, educational technology, and more information. There are newsletters relating to special education, global education, K-12, K-16, K-8 parents, STEM-specific, teachers, language education, and educational leaders. The entire list is much longer.

I have not found a more useful way to keep on top of Zoom Learning than by subscribing (free, with no hooks) to Smart-Brief.com's series of newsletters. Each emailed newsletter is a grouping of articles, research, or information on a topic. Each topic is presented with a descriptive header, a few lines from the original publication, and if you want more, you just click on it and you get the entire piece. If nothing makes you hungry, you hit delete and move on. It's that easy, but it also tells you what is happening, why, and how.

Oh, by the way, a month after I left the district kids in one school not only could use cell phones in the school, they could check one out in the office if they forgot theirs!

Another broad resource worthy of your consideration are the many monthly magazines and journals designed to share what's new in computers or technology. *Wired, PC Magazine, Gizmag,* and *MacLife* are just a few.

Learn It

Go to school. Take an academy. Start a discussion group. Find out how BYOD works, what Flipped Classrooms are, how group interaction affects achievement, what research tells us about teaching styles, proximity, starting times, class arrangement, and a long list of proven ways to teach more effectively. Each plays a part in the enhancement of Zoom Learning.

Flipped Classes: "Flipped classrooms" are a reversal of the way we traditionally teach. In a flipped classroom the teacher videos the lesson, sends it home for watching, and the students do their homework in the classroom. Thus the "homework" becomes watching the lesson at home (or at a friend's house, or on the bus, or in study hall). And the school time becomes where and when the student does their "homework." Why does this work? Well, since there are many resources on this topic I will thumbnail a few reasons for you, hoping you will do more research. It works because kids are more engaged during the class time and you are there to direct their homework. Kids can help other kids at home or at school. At home they can watch the lesson together, or call each other (or text, email, chat, etc.). They can rewind the lesson and watch it over and over. The lesson at home is about 15-20 minutes as compared to 35-40 minutes in the classroom (no interruptions, no questions, no ramp-up or close-down time, etc.). Homework completion goes up dramatically, achievement goes up as homework goes up, and there is a substantial reduction in discipline! Sound good? For the right subjects it is. There are teaching tactics that need to be learned and the entire process requires a degree of technology understanding. It is also gaining popularity across the country and the teachers who do it, on the average, love it. As do the kids.

When it comes to Zoom Learning, don't just hand off the research and learning duties to others. Get involved. Form committees to tackle improvement, to set up trial programs, to pilot apps, and to do trial runs on new equipment. Train librarians or media specialists to be "retrainers" for the rest of the staff. Invite outside speakers or encourage (assign) teachers to make presentations on teaching tactics that work, or how they incorporate cable TV in the classroom, or how they send home taped programs through the web, or use DVD's and DVD players. Get them to share what works and why.

Do It

Finally, you are the spark plug, the igniter, the one who moves the building from a dead stop to zoom. You inspire, engage, encourage, support, push, expect, and measure the speed of progress, the rate of zoom. Zoom Learning starts with you. If you do your job with zeal, it doesn't end, it keeps on *zooming*!

Chapter 9

Team Leadership

This is not a chapter on teamwork. It is a chapter on team leadership. Semantics? No, there is a huge difference between the two. Participating on a team requires an understanding of teamwork, and what it takes to be a team member. But leading a team? That's a totally different ball game.

When someone goes from the classroom to the office, they also move from team membership to team leadership. Principals may have served time on a curriculum development committee, school improvement plan team, compensation revision commission, or even the faculty softball team—and they may have done a stellar job of fulfilling their role on each. We have all been on a team at some time. Being on a team starts when you are a little kid and goes on until you decide to stop contributing! But leading the team is a job left to those given the responsibility and those who are considered leaders. School administrators immediately find themselves in this role from day one. It can be a new role with an undeveloped skill set, but it is a role that you will do time and time again, and you need to do it well. From faculty meetings to state assessment committees, from special education IEP meetings, to discipline review councils, no matter what you call them, they are teams of people bound by common goals and led by an assigned supervisor—the team leader. In most cases, that's you, the principal. Even if you assign the team an on-site manager, and you lead from afar, you are still a team leader.

Moving from being on the team to leading the team requires a different mindset and a well-developed set of leadership skills. The style of leadership you demonstrate during the school day may be the same style you bring to the team meeting. If it works, it is respected. If it employs the many qualities we have discussed so far regarding leadership, you should be good to go. You see, it is not by chance that this chapter comes near the end of this toolbook. This chapter reflects and puts to use a number of the things we have previously discussed.

What Is a Team?

During many training sessions with new administrators it has become quite clear that the concepts of teams, teamwork, and team leadership are often excluded from administrative preparation courses. In fact, it's even a bit foreign to many who enter the ranks of administration. So, before we dig in, let's be sure we understand a few of the basics. For instance, how is a team defined?

A team is

* a group of people who compete in a sport, game, etc., against another group;
* a group of two or more animals used to pull a wagon, cart, etc., and—*most important for our purposes*—
* a group of people who work together.

The common phrase, obviously, is "a group of..." And when you bring "a group" of people together you have a mix of personalities, emotions, agendas, schedules, abilities, values, and of course, motivation. There are many other factors that might influence the attitude or energy of team members, such as families, work, health, and much more. All of these factors affect a person's ability or desire to serve and how to contribute to the team. Thus, as the leader, you have to understand, compensate for, and balance every individual's contribution and how their respective skills and idiosyncrasies affect the mix. So one skill that is needed right from the very beginning is the ability to recognize differences in individuals and then find how to balance the many energies and inputs to move the team forward.

Team Strength

The concept of two of more animals forming a "team" always reminds me of the facts you learn in grade school that state how much stronger two animals are when working to-gether than the two same animals working alone. Or the strength of two cords wrapped together compared to a single cord, or how exponentially the strength increases with the ad-dition of more cords, or more animals. As a young science teacher I always loved demonstrating the power of "teaming" things together. It is indeed amazing.

But with people it is harder to measure. Five players on a basketball team can be greatly influenced by one inept player, when maybe four would work better. So numbers don't guar-antee greatness when it comes to *human* teams. What does make a difference is leadership. The coach, or team leader, is the one who aligns the talents, plays the strength, benches the weakness, and employs choice and direction in making the team successful. You can have a team of five excellent athletes who perform far below their potential, not because of their talents, but in direct response to their leadership. The same is true with a team of teachers. So skill number two is the under-standing that if you lead the team to work together, it becomes strong and powerful.

Team Selection

As a principal you will form many teams. Some are formed by default, such as faculty members as a whole, or people se-lected by an outside agency or the central office. You may lead a team of parents and teachers working on the school disci-pline code, and may have only selected one or two of the members, with the others gifts from the superintendent, other administrators, or the president of the PTO. Sometimes you must take what is given to you, and then work your leadership magic.

Remember, however, that when *you* pick the team, the quality of the membership is the most important indicator of the team's success. It's the very reason why we have such in-volved and detailed drafting systems for professional sports teams, why we go through the rigor of hiring the best people, why we train and mold building leaders to work well with dis-trict administration—all because the team's success is directly related to the quality of the members *and the team's leadership.* It's also important to remember that you float to the top when a team succeeds, and fall when the team fails. So skill number three is to carefully select the best team possible. Or, when the team is handed to you, learn individual skills and talents so you can weave the individuals into a solid unit.

So how do you select quality teams? A very interesting and somewhat odd book (by Sheldon Bowles, Richard Silvano, and Susan Silvano) called *Kingdomality* changed the way I thought about team selection. The book is too quirky to quickly summarize but the message it conveys is substantial. It says, in a nutshell, that there are many personality types (it outlines 12). It then says that team leaders should not pick teams based on a preconceived notion that people want to serve, they will contribute, or are even the right people. You need to pick teams carefully knowing and thinking about the personalities of the potential members.

One example is a principal selecting a committee (or team) to review and recommend a textbook series for upper elementary social studies. Traditionally one would select the fourth-, fifth- and sixth-grade teachers, possibly a building administrator, maybe even a central office curriculum specialist. Also considered might be someone from the primary school or the middle school, for purposes of articulation. This seems reasonable, and without any training you might think that all these people would have some skin in the game and would love to serve on this team. Remember that this team might meet 6-10 times with textbook reps, to discuss options, to look at peripheral curriculum, and then to spend extra hours reading and reviewing literature. It's a lot of work, so you want people who are dedicated, committed, and even excited.

So if you just appoint the obvious folks you might not get the best team with the highest level of interest, especially if folks selected don't give a hoot about social studies or really care about what series is selected. *Kingdomality* says to pick people of varying skills, various talents, and *all with an interest.* Pick people who want to serve and can contribute to the process.

Does this mean the administrator puts up a sign-up sheet and asks anyone interested to join the fun? I think you know the answer to that one. You still have to invite and/or select members to the team, but this time you interview them about their input or expertise, giving them an option to join or not to join. Certainly you know some of the key players that you want and you will invite them with a degree of need, encouragement, and enthusiasm. You might also remember, or be told, that the custodian is a history buff, even a Civil War re-enactor. He may absolutely love to have input on the committee, and with a son in sixth grade, he might actually be very familiar with the current offerings. You might also find that the prominent, highly regarded fifth-grade teacher that you rely on for all things wonderful, may truly love math and science and have a passion for reading and language, but silently loathes anything to do with social studies. You think, "I would be remiss not putting her on the committee." Then when you ask her if she wants to serve, rather than just assigning her, you learn she would opt for root canal surgery first. Good to know because you want a quality committee.

The process of selecting the right committee members employs your communication skills, your personal leadership style, your intuitive problem-solving abilities, and other "natural" skills you exhibit (or learn).

The acronym KING is used in the book *Kingdomality*. The K stands for Know Yourself and Know Others. The I is to identify the issues. N means to name your team. G means get goals and get going. These are great thoughts for picking the best folks to do the best job.

The bottom line: spend a lot of time selecting a team that will work together, has interest in the subject, and wants to be there. And use all you know about leadership to build and steer the team.

The Big Team

One of my personal passions working in the field of education is the concept that all partners should be on the same "big" team. Few things are more important than education. It is right up there with your family, your health, and your values. Education is the key to everything.

Let me set the stage about the big team of education. An educated person has the opportunity to open most doors. The causal effect of education on earnings is tremendous. Recent reports from the National Center for Education Statistics indicate that a 25 to 34-year-old (in 2011) earned an average of $59,200 with a master's degree education, $45,000 with a bachelor's degree, $37,000 with an associate's degree, $30,000 with a high school diploma, and $22,900 for those who never graduated from high school. The more education you get, the more you earn.

Similar statistics can be found comparing the number of unemployed people and their accomplished level of education.

Have I told you anything you don't already know? Of course I haven't. But if this information is so widely available, and so universally understood, then why isn't education *truly* the number one priority of legislators, government, and everyone? The data demonstrates that investing in our education results in more taxes paid in and less expenditure for government assistance paid out. Education also has a relationship with certain forms of cancer, obesity, and other high-cost illnesses and diseases. In fact, you can relate the value of education with crime, drugs, and almost all negative social ills. So, again I ask, why aren't schools our number one priority?

Maybe one of the reasons is that we don't always play nice inside the system. We don't work as a "big" team. A team that consists of everyone who believes in the value of education. That certainly includes those who have chosen education as their profession and passion. And, as you read in Chapter 3, that also includes everyone in the education family. Then add to the "big" team students, parents, and all the taxpayers.

If then we believe that education itself is a "team activity," we need to work toward that end with excellent team leadership. That means leading our schools to be more education-focused and more student-directed, with the goal of producing well-educated and contributing members of society. We do this by leading the troops to earn the role of respected and admired professionals. Principals can accomplish this by replacing the concept of "negotiations" with "discussions." By replacing union mentality with professional responsibility. It means that boards need to recognize the importance of the teaching team and the teachers need to recognize the value and significance of the elected team, by appreciating that both are on the same team, meaning the same side. When we do that, when we become members of one team, working together, we will change everything for the better.

So how does the principal lead this team? Easy. Look for situations in your school or district that don't support the "big" team concept. Maybe it is a traditional divide between teachers and administration, salaries and the board, state revenue and needs, unwanted or misunderstood federal mandates, or something as simple as the high school not willing to work with the grade school. Ask why, seek the reasons, and introduce a change. Share the "big" team mindset and slowly but consistently put it in place. From the chapter on Vision, couldn't this be a vision that you start—and then transplant for ownership?

I love the story of the school principal who went head-to-head with a rift between two wings of her building. One wing was the upper elementary section, grades 5 and 6. The other wing was the traditional junior high section, grades 7 and 8. About the only thing they shared was a common cafeteria. For years the teachers from one wing were envious of the teachers in the other wing. It was such an entrenched dislike that no one could really tell you why or how it began. The principal believed in the "big" team concept and decided to form a "Collaboration Committee" for the purpose of moving the students (5-8) to a higher level of achievement and recognition. She wanted to establish a "brand" for her school, as one school, not two wings. She spent considerable time selecting, and then inviting, nine people to serve on this team. She purposefully selected a teacher new to the system from each wing, a few crusty veterans, and one or two crossovers who taught in both wings. She made sure there were some "old school" and "bold school" folks represented as well. All nine folks that she asked agreed, although she will readily admit that some agreed with great trepidation. The principal certainly employed powerful communication skills during the recruitment process!

She then employed her best leadership skills in having them set defined goals for student improvement, and before you knew it, it meant that they needed to work together as one school, not two wings. They confirmed that the articulation between sixth and seventh grade was lacking and needed to be reinforced. They also agreed that in order to produce a "brand" they needed to best understand the specifics of how each "wing" operated. One meeting after another brought these nine staff members (ten with the leader) together as a true team. They became excited about working side by side, and they set up many activities that broke the long-standing barriers of not just working together, but respecting each other.

I can honestly tell you that single-handedly the principal engaged the talents of the nine individual team members to turn the entire culture of the school from two entities into one hugely successful, fully cooperative schoolhouse. The momentum grew with each meeting, and when the task seemed to be near completion, the team decided to remain intact and found new challenges to overcome.

Finally, when it comes to the "big" team, the more we talk about and market our needs as educators, the more we emphasize that we are all on the same side, providing an education for every child. And the more we are willing to *face and defeat negativity* in the profession, the better we serve. Team leaders can make this happen.

Ten Rules

"Simple Truths" is a series of excellent books on a variety of topics including all phases of leadership and management. One of my favorites is a book called *Pulling Together* by John J. Murphy. In this book, the author gives ten rules for high-performance team leadership. I would like to share these rules and give you my paraphrased, personal description of each one. I have also found that reviewing this list is very helpful when any team is newly formed. It provides a common basis of expectations to each member.

Rule #1: Put the Team First
This means "me" becomes "we." I take myself out of the role of being the boss, or being the resource, or being in charge and move into the role of being one of many—putting the team before myself. Even the leader must set aside their role as the director and become a facilitator. Of course when readjustments are needed, the team leader gently moves the team back in the right direction.

Rule #2: Communicate Openly and Candidly
You will help the team if you are honest while remaining professional and tactful. If you don't understand something, say so. If you have fears, express them. If there is information to share that may be negative but is important, don't hold back. Just employ your ability to be honest, tactful, and careful. In other words, be sure to share what you feel, what you don't understand, and what might also be on the minds of many. Learn to lead with patience, humility, and kindness. Remember the arrow dipped in honey?

Rule #3: Be Part of the Solution, Not the Problem
Don't add drama or stress to the team. Be thoughtful about your role and appreciate the impact your comments may have or your impatience may bring. The team was put together to solve an issue, be proactive to possible concerns, or offer answers to questions. When you stray from the role of solving or answering a question, you take the team off center. So, be hon-

est and follow Rule #2, but also be productive and helpful. If there is one rule that team leaders need to learn, it is to lead with strength *and with calmness*—a blend that when mixed together correctly is very productive.

Rule #4: Respect Diversity

This is an essential. The team may be assembled for the very reason that divergent views are needed, or that hearing more than one viewpoint is the best way to find the best solution. In the process you may run into religious, political, or racial differences that test your tolerance. You may be a Yankee fan in a room full of Red Sox fans. No matter what, you must respect diversity and actually embrace what it brings to the team

Rule #5: Ask and Encourage the Right Questions

I once participated in a strategic planning process with a "team" of about thirty folks from the district and community. One lady, a parent and businesswoman, was invited to be part of the team for her widely respected success, and her long-standing work with the band parents. During the two days we met she didn't say five words. When we were consummating the process and listing the agreed-upon strategies, she raised her hand and said she didn't understand one of the major and fundamental concepts we had discussed ad nauseam. If there was ever a time I wanted to have a Taser gun with me it was then, but that would probably be in direct violation of Rule #7, so I politely responded and a handful of people spent several minutes answering a question that should have been asked several hours earlier—or the day before. You respect the members of the team when you ask and encourage others to ask the right questions, at the right time. A good leader keeps reminding the team of this, and keeps asking if everyone is on target.

Rule #6: Use a Rational Problem-Solving Process

There are many types of problem-solving processes available, just Google it and a thousand will jump on your screen. OK, maybe a dozen. The point is that you don't have to fly by the seat of your pants when in comes to finding a doable and reasonable problem-solving process. When I facilitate strategic planning I have a very basic one I use that involves posing a question, having small groups answer it, reporting to the large group, and using consensus to reach a group answer. If you don't have a well-defined, rule-infused process... expect mayhem. And with no process the type A folks take over and the wallflowers wilt. Find a process, share it, and then facilitate its magic. A good leader finds a way to make the process owned and used by the members.

Rule #7: Build Trust with Integrity and Example

Simply stated, be a good soldier. Stay calm and professional. Be the example of arriving on time, turning your phone to vibrate, working hard, and making a great impression. Be a patient and compassionate leader. Yes, this means no Taser guns.

Rule #8: Commit to Excellence

You might not hit 10 out of 10 on the excitement chart with the topic or the time involved, but no matter what, commit your talent, time, and input toward an excellent process and result. Make it work by making it the number one priority and working at it like it is the best thing ever. And, strive for the best solutions ever. As the team leader *your* excitement will become contagious.

Rule #9: Promote Interdependent Thinking

This means to encourage give-and-take. Accept advice and information, and share it. Offer it when leadership calls. Become involved with the group and "feel" the teamwork. I have been on some organizations that did a great job building this *interdependent* bond. I have been on teams that did not, and when the teamwork was over, it was just over. Good teamwork can produce excellent and meaningful results, and it can be great fun as well. When it really clicks you build relationships as well as solve problems. Team leaders facilitate this by matching up people within the group, by promoting fun when needed, by asking good questions that encourage discussion and interaction.

The School Principal's Toolbook

Rule #10: Pull the Weeds

I like to think this rule applies more to the leader than the team—that's you. As a team leader you need to know when to make necessary changes, rearrange participants, talk privately to someone who is taking over and not being a good team player, or when to redirect or realign the team for the good of the process. Pull the weeds means to keep the process moving, and to keep it clean of distractions or distracters. Not always fun, but always important.

That's it: ten rules to make the team highly effective through great team leadership. Again, sharing these rules at the onset can help set the stage for success.

The Team Player

John Maxwell wrote a wonderful book that I recommend to every team leader. It is *The 17 Essential Qualities of a Team Player*. I love this book for one simple reason: it hits the target dead center. If you are leading a team, if you understand the "Rules for Highly Effective Teamwork" that we just discussed, then you are primed to pass out this book and let all your teachers and team members read Maxwell's words. These qualities extend far beyond just teamwork, they also outline the qualities needed to be a part of the school family

Here are the qualities as presented by Maxwell:

(1) Adaptable: If you won't change for the team, the team may change you.
(2) Collaborative: Working together precedes winning together.
(3) Committed: There are no halfhearted champions
(4) Communicative: A team is many voices with a single heart.
(5) Competent: If you can't, your team won't.
(6) Dependable: Teams go to "go-to" players.
(7) Disciplined: Where there's a will, there's a win.
(8) Enlarging: Adding value to teammates is invaluable.
(9) Enthusiastic: Your heart is the source of energy for the team.

(10) Intentional: Make every action count.

(11) Mission Conscious: The big picture is coming in loud and clear.

(12) Prepared: Preparation can mean the difference between winning and losing.

(13) Relational: If you get along, others will go along.

(14) Self-Improving: To improve the team, improve yourself.

(15) Selfless: There is no "I" in team.

(16) Solution Oriented: Make a resolution to find the solution.

(17) Tenacious: Never, never, never quit.

And while these are qualities or characteristics of a good team *member*, they are even more important for the team *leader*.

Professional Learning Communities

Rick DuFour is a name that most professional educators have seen or know. He is one of the fathers of the professional learning community (PLC) concept. I have had the opportunity to work with Rick and his staff and to see firsthand some of the many accomplishments a professional learning community can produce. I encourage principals to investigate and learn about PLCs. And developing a PLC means forming many teams that evaluate needs, develop procedures, and make changes. It is firmly rooted in the team process.

Rick has made the following statement many times, "There is abundant research linking higher levels of student achievement to educators who work in the collaborative culture of a professional learning community." A highly effective principal builds collaboration by bringing professionals together to solve problems, discuss issues, and, together, move the school forward. It has to do with teamwork. It is successful because of team leadership.

Finally

Henry Ford said, "You will find men who want to be carried on the shoulders of others, who think that the world owes them a living. They don't seem to see that we must all lift together and pull together." When we work together we are stronger than when we work as individuals. When we can professionally muster our talents and funnel them into an agreed-upon force, we can change anything. When we seek and find the "big" team, we will indeed change the world. And it all starts with one person. Guess who that may be?

Chapter 10

Expert Advice

I'm a firm believer in asking for help. I've done it all my life, professional and personal. I'm also a guy that doesn't believe in reinventing the wheel. I may try to make it better, but first I try to learn from those who have "been there, done that." So, when I try to share my expertise or personal opinions, I seek the wisdom of those I respect and admire, those who have been in the field; those who have walked the walk.

In this chapter I am sharing the responses from a variety of esteemed professionals. Some have been nationally recognized, some are respected peers I worked with side by side, but all share a common characteristic, they have been exceptional building leaders. They know how to make a difference.

I asked each "expert" two questions:

1. What are the most important qualities of a school leader?
2. What skills are needed to achieve a level of administrative excellence?

As you can imagine, talented and creative people respond in many different ways. I expected a variety of answers and was not disappointed. Still, you will see many fundamental similarities in their responses.

I also put this chapter near the end of this book so that you might be able to weave what we have talked about into the responses from these esteemed leaders. You should be building a common core (oops, I'm sorry, it just slipped out) of shared beliefs and ideas about the challenges and needs of being a highly effective leader.

I've chosen leaders whose advice should be heard, mostly because of their successful careers and the respect they have earned as educational leaders. All these "experts" were or are principals. They represent many different schools and states but they share one important characteristic, they are A leaders in making a difference for kids. I have learned a great deal from their leadership and collaboration through the years.

I purposely selected professionals that I know, with personalities that I can honestly say I admire. They are real leaders, coming from real histories, and are in the profession not to advance themselves, but to advance the profession through kids.

I have divided their responses into two sections: *Qualities* first, followed by *Skills*. I will introduce them to you when you first meet them. When they are done sharing we can talk some more.

I hope you enjoy and learn from their words...

Qualities of Effective Building Leaders

* **Jason Leahy** *is a bright, energetic young father of five. He served as a high school teacher, principal of two high schools, and is currently the executive director of the Illinois Principals Association with over 4,700 hundred members and 23 employees. I know Jason personally and did the homework to hire him as a principal in my last district. If I had to define him in one word it would be* **"exceptional."** *He represents the best of the best. Jason Leahy is a name most of us will know at some point in our educational administrative journey.*

Jason lists the following five areas as the most important characteristics of a building leader:

Lead Yourself Well First

Imagine the leadership qualities and characteristics you possess as being contained in an internal cup. Those who choose to follow you can only "drink" from the overflow you provide. This requires that you be a learner and make your leadership "cup" overflow by being a voracious reader, meeting with mentors, attending to relevant professional development, connecting with peers, and staying dialed in to the latest developments in the field. Much of this can be accomplished through membership in your requisite principals association. And, did I mention read a lot? Leaders are readers.

Be Humble

You are not perfect. You do not know everything. Be very good at saying you are sorry even when what you are apologizing for is not directly your fault or the fault of anyone in your school. Give credit where credit is due. Be willing to shoulder the blame. You are the leader. Good ones know that this comes with the territory. Humility will take you a long way to building trust and getting buy-in for the vision you possess for your school.

Have Integrity

Always choose to do what is right, ethical, and legal. When you make a mistake, see "Be Humble."

Love People, Especially Kids

Leading a school would be easy if it weren't for people. People make things hard. People make things messy. As the head of your school, you will have people coming to you with their baggage and their problems. Do the best you can to help them resolve those issues. People, especially kids, need for you to be patient and love them through difficult circumstances. If you find yourself unable to love people, find something else to do. You are in the wrong business.

Be a Servant

School leadership is all about being "other minded." Are you working to create a safe environment for kids to learn? Are you working to provide teachers the resources they need to be successful in the classroom? Are you helping parents to problem solve and identify resources to assist a problem child? A commitment to serving others and meeting their needs is where the real reward of school leadership lies. Grab it!

-----

* **Dr. Jane Westerhold** *has been there. She has served as a teacher, assistant principal, principal in several schools, and now superintendent of one of the best elementary districts in the country. I know because I proudly went to school in the Des*

Plaines Community Consolidated School District #62. Jane has earned many prestigious awards, the most recent being named the 2013 Superintendent of the Year in Illinois. My one word description for Jane is **"visionary."** *She knows how to lead, how to "see ahead," and how to bring the best out of those who serve.*

Jane shared the following characteristics of a school leader:

* Leadership is having some sort of influence over others.
* Leaders (and managers) are predisposed to excel in one area or another (leadership or management).
* Non-negotiable characteristics of all leaders are honesty, integrity, trustworthiness, and general intelligence, plus cognitive capacities, strong moral compass, and being honorable and confident.
* Added characteristics of leaders moving to a higher level of effectiveness are strong moral fiber, intestinal fortitude, stoutheartedness (grit), creativity, willingness to take risks, curiosity, hunger for new knowledge, a DNA for continuous improvement, intuitiveness, imagination, perception, resilience, possessing an entrepreneurial spirit, caring, perseverance, and having empathy for others.

-----

* **Dr. Lane Abrell** *has a long history of serving kids. He has been a teacher, dean, assistant principal, principal, associate superintendent, and now superintendent of one of the largest school districts in Illinois. Lane received the honor of being named the Illinois High School Principal of the Year. My word for Lane is* **"effective."** *No matter where Lane goes, he leads a team that makes a difference.*

Lane lists the three top qualities for effective building leaders as: (1) integrity, (2) honesty, and a (3) strong work ethic.

(I could also describe Lane as *brief!*)

The School Principal's Toolbook

* **Julie Korte** *is nothing short of a gem. By choice she has remained at the helm of a primary school for 15 years as the principal. She loves what she does. Prior to serving as principal she was an outstanding elementary teacher. She has the ability to select, mentor, lead, and develop some of the best teachers that have ever existed. She leads quietly but with high expectations. She exhibits all the qualities that you will read about in this book. My one word for Julie is* **"determined."**

Julie shares the following characteristics: the school leader must be flexible, patient, compassionate, approachable, intelligent, healthy, dedicated, child-centered, empathetic, positive; have a good sense of humor; be fun-loving, even-tempered, kind, and service oriented.

-----

* **Dan Grandame** *shares some of the same characteristics as Julie Korte. Following an exceptional teaching career at the elementary level, Dan served 17 years in the role of principal. He coached and served his community in many capacities and was a hands-on leader. Every student knew and loved Dan, and every parent respected him. He truly cared about each and every person in his building, the child, employee, or guest. A team player in every respect, but there was never a doubt in his leadership style that the needs of the "kiddos," as he called them, were always first. My word for Dan is* **"loving."**

Here is what Dan says about the characteristics of an excellent leader:

1. Character, the mental and moral qualities distinctive to an individual. Character speaks volumes about what any school leader needs. Knowledge is important, but the leader must possess high moral standards and have a strong moral compass.
2. The leader must be an excellent communicator in both oral and written communications.
3. The leader must possess the ability to be very highly organized—a person that doesn't procrastinate or wait until the last minute to complete assignments, appointments, etc.

The School Principal's Toolbook

4. Caring and empathy are also very important.

-----

* **Brad Albrecht.** *I admire this guy beyond words. We worked together as teachers, coaches, even as summer maintenance men and painters. We held ladders for each other as we painted gyms, houses, or barns. I was Brad's principal and superintendent, and then he followed me as principal and superintendent in the same district. I'd like to think that I mentored him in some ways, but truth be told I learned from his devotion, commitment, and style. He was a great coach, a great teacher, and will always be a great administrator. He is the only person I know to have a gymnasium named after him while still the school leader. I'm not very objective when it comes to Brad. My assessment of his talents is widely shared by those fortunate enough to have worked for him, learned because of him, and called him a friend. My word for Brad is simply* "**amazing.**"

Brad says the following about school leadership:

The school leader provides leadership by informing and engaging others and by empowering teachers through dedication and strength. The leader must be proactive, have a vision, and think win/win. Parents need to know that the leader is there for student growth and for the learning process.

-----

* **Dr. Rick Acuncius** *has a long list of credentials. Rick's professional career includes teacher, talented musician, middle school principal, and now college professor. Rick was a leader with the middle school professional organization and led the middle school movement throughout the country by example and leadership. He earned many awards of recognition including the Milken National Educator Award, Illinois Middle School Principal of the Year, and several State Awards of Excellence. He also led many teachers to be recognized as award winners in various curricular roles, National Board Certification, or in other excep-*

tional capacities. He was instrumental in developing one of the first joint consumer education/technology labs in the country. His leadership was founded on his vision and understanding of the needs of his students. One word to describe his leadership would be "inspirational." Rick inspired change, vision, and learning every day for teachers and students.

Characteristics:

Know Thyself
Know your strengths and weaknesses, and utilize the strengths of others. Bring in team members whose strengths differ from yours.

Communication
Know when to listen, when to be quiet, and how to communicate.

Visibility, Accessibility, Approachability
Greet students in the morning, when you can, and by name, if you can.

Help People Grow
Focus on the positive and then work on the negative so it does not become criticism but an observation of how one can grow.

Do As I Say and As I Do
Be a role model of the extra effort of putting your family first, of displaying of a balance between faith, family, and the job.

Be Honest
If you don't have an answer, admit it, then find it.

Know Your "Formal Role"
Be sure everyone knows you are part of the district, but not the final answer. Encourage working together.

-----

* Dr. Fred Singleton *achieved a milestone that few educators can attain: he has served the profession for 50 years. Fred started as a teacher and coach. He served as an assistant principal and then principal of a very high-achieving high school for 14*

The School Principal's Toolbook

years. When he retired from working in the field, he moved to the position of director for the Illinois Principals Association, serving in many capacities for 20 years. During his long and esteemed career Fred was recognized many times for his talents and leadership. One of the most influential roles Fred served was directing and formulating professional development for building-level administrators, professional development that made a difference and certainly elevated the skills and talents of thousands of administrators. I can't give Fred one word, it has to be two: **"difference maker."** In addition, Fred has always been a thinker, and always provided a varied and interesting perspective.

Fred's response to the question about qualifications is as follows:

My point of reference is from being an administrator, watching great presenters, and attending professional development opportunities.

My first observation is that in calling the principal a "leader," using the term "leader" assumes that there will be people following. New and experienced building administrators need to periodically turn around to check to see if anyone is actually following the principal's lead or are they just talking the talk but not walking the walk. Therefore, I prefer the term guide (showing the way, not necessarily the front person). God did not suddenly give the person sitting in the administrator's chair the only wisdom. There are lots of capable individuals on the staff who can provide assistance. With that said, my most important characteristic for the quality "leader" is to develop *trust.*

Trust: with staff, students, parents, the superintendent, the board of education, and finally the community. It takes all of the parties to trust each other. A quality principal, as soon as he/she takes the position, must begin work on building, brick by brick and action by action, the network of trust. If the administrator has little or no credibility, things will not get done efficiently—each decision will be met with a challenge.

"Respect is earned, honesty is appreciated, trust is gained. Loyalty is returned."

The School Principal's Toolbook

A leader does lead, but more importantly they guide their school; they check to see if anyone is behind them, they communicate expectations, they model those expectations, they ask questions, and then they listen. They gather information before reacting.

A quality principal comes to the job with these qualities: compassion, desire, ethics, honesty, and a strong desire to make changes that improve opportunities.

-----

* **Andy Carmitchel:** *Andy is the last "expert" I will introduce, but certainly not last in the influence he has had on education throughout his career. Andy was an English teacher, and then served as a school administrator for 25 of his 35 years in the trenches. Most of his service was as a high school principal, with some years as the middle school leader. He served as an assistant superintendent for four years. Now he is an accomplished author and consummate fan of the Chicago Cubs. Bravo for your conviction and devotion! Andy's leadership was exceptional. He set expectations and then helped his staff and students achieve them. He could articulate, demonstrate, and congratulate achievement. My one word for Andy is* **"leader."**

Here is Andy's list of characteristics shared by outstanding educational leaders:

An outstanding school administrator knows that as long as the goal is reached, it doesn't matter who gets the credit.

She knows that for any innovation or idea to be effectively implemented there must be "buy-in" by the implementers. They must own it. Ideally, in the end, the implementers won't remember whose idea it was in the first place, and she won't remind them. She'll be too busy celebrating the success with them.

The administrator is both open-minded and decisive. These traits are not opposites. They intertwine. She knows to listen to all, and to display the same level of intense interest and respect to each one (the good ideas and the ludicrous ones), then deliberate and decide. She will announce a decision with a tone of finality, but one imbued with a strong rationale, as well as a respect for all.

The administrator is always acting one step ahead but thinking three steps ahead.

While deadly serious about providing the best education possible for the kids in her charge, she never stops looking for ways to have fun. Never. And she doesn't care if she's the butt of the joke. She knows joy is a magic elixir when added to work.

She really cares. Really. All the time.

The administrator has, imbedded inside her, a deep, strong, unshakable set of values; a clear set of principles that she lives by. This inner core is infused with compassion, humility and respect for all. But when she sees something is wrong, it's wrong, and it will not stand. Not on her watch.

And finally, this administrator never quits learning. She'll never quit reading, never quit sharing, and never quit listening.

And she never quits smiling, inside or out.

Skills

You've met our team of experts, and in so doing you see why I specifically chose them. They are a mixed bag of leadership, each with their own style and brand of expertise. I loved sharing their backgrounds with you because I know the impact each has had on principals across our country. They represent what this book is all about—*developing the talent within you*. No two of you will be the same, and like our panel of experts, you will influence our profession uniquely, and I hope masterfully. Just as each person you just met became a true representative of exceptional building leadership, I hope you will take a piece of each one as you build your story and your influence. Some of the experts are still working hard doing their jobs, but all of them, no matter what they are doing, have been masterful leaders.

Let's hear from them again, this time as they share what they feel are the most important skills for an effective building leader.

* **Dr. Lane Abrell** lists the following as necessary skills: (1) ability to "check your ego at the door" and to "treat everyone like they are famous," (2) strong communication skills (including listening), (3) ability to be visible while still meeting office deadlines, (4) ability and willingness to network with colleagues outside the building and district, and (5) ability to think on your feet.

-----

* **Jason Leahy** lists three skills as being the top on his list:

Relationship Building
There may not be a truer leadership cliché than, "People don't care how much you know until you know how much you care." Students, teachers, parents, and community members must know that they can trust you before they will be willing to follow you where you want to go.

Time & Task Management
Not many jobs put as many demands on one's time or require one to monitor as many moving parts as a principal. Leaders who are not effective at managing their time and an ever-mounting pile of tasks will find their credibility evaporate— fast. It is critical to find a system, written or digital, that helps you stay on top of things.

You cannot share your vision as well as expectations for performance without outstanding written and oral communication skills. In addition to more traditional means of communicating, you have to leverage available social medias (i.e., Twitter, Facebook, etc.) to meet your audience where they are and stay relevant.

-----

* **Dr. Jane Westerhold** says the following about skills:

Skills can be acquired. Some are basic and may not move the organization forward, but are fundamental and expected: strong communication skills that encompass written, oral, and listening; ability to solve problems, make and implement decisions, set goals, build trust, use common sense when making decisions; organization and time management skills.

To advance the school the following skills are needed: ability to inspire, persuade, and motivate. To be able to paint a vision of the future that cannot be seen, one must practice lifelong learning, articulate vision to stakeholders, and, if in the central office, demonstrate a global perspective of the district.

Also needed is the skill of reflection in order to learn, change, and grow.

-----

* **Dan Grandame's** list of most important skills include:

1. Knowledge of new learning standards: the ability to not only know them, but be able to articulate them to staff, parents, and see to it that the students achieve high standards in mastery of the learning standards.
2. Time-management skills
3. Strong leadership skills
4. Self-motivation and being able to positively motivate others

Also, Dan states that the effective educational leader needs to love kids and be willing to do whatever it takes to help them become lifelong learners and excellent citizens, with high moral and ethical standards, and be empathetic to all.

-----

* **Julie Korte** lists these as the most important skills:

Good time management. Able to organize, multi-task, and communicate. Aware of current technology, able to use technology to become more efficient, are a people person, see things from another's perspective, can interview, able to identify when a lesson falls short and to lead a teacher to do the same, analyze data, help teachers analyze data, create schedules, read a situation, make good decisions, manage crises, give specific feedback, stay focused on a vision, make a tough con-

The School Principal's Toolbook

versation palatable, stay calm, manage stress, prioritize (knowing what battles are worth fighting), and give the benefit of the doubt. And, are able to pick teams carefully and ask your teachers when you have questions (using their expertise).

-----

* **Brad Albrecht** lists these as the top skills needed by a school leader:

1. Take ownership
2. Motivate staff and students
3. Communicate with all stakeholders
4. Lead by example
5. Be flexible
6. Have trust in others

Brad also feels that ownership covers a lot of territory. A good leader knows what is happening and is a part of the total program.

-----

* **Rick Acuncius'** list of skills: Be a communicator and listener, know your people, be a lifelong learner, don't take yourself too seriously knowing that someday you will be replaced. Know your values, know how to work with people who are structured differently than you, know that you don't need to know all the answers. Find a mentor. Don't take undue criticism, but act on appropriate criticism. Use tools to help: Bolman and Deal's *Four Frames of Leadership* helped me learn how to solve problems through structural and human resources and political and symbolic frames. Use tools.

-----

* **Dr. Fred Singleton** says that the administrator needs these skills to be a quality leader:

1. Must be able to transmit the vision/mission to all educational parties; creates a buy-in on the focus of the school.
2. Must be able to distinguish who are the explorers, pioneers, and settlers on the staff to make changes: Explorers are just a few who will venture out to the edge and experiment, unafraid of failure. The pioneers will be the ones who will develop the building blocks to encourage the settlers to come. Finally, the settlers will get on board when they feel they are safe; they do not like lots of change.
3. Know who the "Boss Cow" on the faculty. In a dairy herd there is always one cow that leads the rest to the barn. If she does not go, the others will wait as well. Changes in school situations will not fare well unless the key teacher is on board. The new principal needs to listen and observe before making changes.
4. Continue to grow professionally. When you stop learning you are finished as a leader. Educators are either like wine or bread. The older they get, the better they get, like fine wine, or the older they get, the staler they get, like week-old bread. The principal must be fresh by belonging to professional associations, exploring new educational concepts, talking with principals experiencing success, and by encouraging faulty to think outside the box in teaching.
5. Always keep your superintendent informed of any alligators in the swamp, and of proposed changes. Remember that "loyalty" is not a word, it is a lifestyle.
6. Take care of yourself regarding your health and family.
7. Make decisions based on your number one goal: is it good for the students?
8. Be willing to give up being in constant control. There are other capable people who can be in charge. It's not wrong because someone does it a different way with the same results.

-----

* Andy Carmitchel says these administrative skills are "the ones you gotta have!"

The School Principal's Toolbook

The skill set(s) that one must develop to become an effective, successful administrator can seem overwhelming. At first, it can be like trying to hit a golf ball right after getting too much advice: you can be trying so hard to remember everything that you're supposed to do with your hands, eyes, arms, feet, and hips that you miss the stupid ball.

The complexities that you'll face in the world of school administration can be like that. You'll be asked, for instance, to be strong, yet compassionate; to be open-minded and yet decisive; and do that all at the same time. There's a lot that seems contradictory. It's a subtle mix that you'll learn. But it *ain't* easy.

There is, however, a good place to start. Below I've identified five skill set areas that I have seen in every outstanding administrator that I've worked with in my career. Though every educational leader is different, the truly effective ones all had these core skill sets in their bag of tricks (I was going to call them the *Common Core*, but I think somebody already used that.) Without further ado:

1. Ability to Motivate

I put this first because everything else doesn't work if you don't have it; or don't develop it. Motivating students and staff to strive to meet ambitious yet achievable goals is the most important thing you can do. Do whatever it takes, and make it fun. Be ready to repeat and repeat, be ready to do handstands, be ready to lavishly celebrate even a modicum of success, then be ready to do it again the next day. Administrators need to think about ways to motivate as much (or more) than they do about law and order. It's how you build an effective team and an effective school.

2. Intuitive Intelligence

I know what you're thinking, "Well, that leaves me out." Not so fast. By "intuitive intelligence" I mean the ability to analyze people or situations so that you can logically predict the outcome, and then, if need be, intervene to change it. This is a learned skill, and a vital one. Example: a high school science department that has half the students that the math department has, and gives out a much lower overall grade point average. It took two years of work (and we had to make them think it was their idea), but the whole department got revamped, and a lot more kids are in science now. Or, on an individual level, for example, looking at a student's predictive failure pattern, and setting up a team intervention. An administrator can and must develop the skill to see the problem ahead of time, then gather the facts about it, analyze it, and help solve it. That's intuitive intelligence.

3. Loving kids

What? Loving as a "skill set"? Ridiculous! Come on, everybody loves kids, right? Nope. Love is like the patience we try so hard to keep, only deeper. It is like faith. It's there, but you've got to work at it sometimes. To truly love each kid that walks through the school door, every day, is a real, developed skill set, baby. To learn to love all of them—the ones who hate you, ignore you, or like you well enough to hug you (but forgot, again, to take a bath the night before)—takes all you can muster up sometimes. The best administrators I've seen all loved unconditionally, but don't think it didn't take work. Feeling genuine compassion for all is a learned skill set. Can't find it in the book. It grows in the heart.

4. An Even Temperament (No Matter What)

You'll need a tough hide around that big heart. The ability not to lose their cool, or their measured judgment, in the face of crises, shouting, cursing, injuries or—surprise—fire alarms is a skill that all the best have. I certainly don't mean to imply that they were born unflappable. This is a learned skill set of the highest order. An administrator has to know that they are in the eye of every storm, and that that eye is being watched all the time. The ability to keep your cool, or to appear to be keeping it, when all hell is breaking loose takes practice. Temper tantrums and panic are not options for a leader. All the great ones know this, or have learned it.

5. An Insatiable Mind

The best ones know that they will never quit learning. All weaknesses can be overcome through knowledge. Great administrators are always reading, sharing, and seeking. Not all of them were always that way, I can assure you. But they *became* that way. They worked at it until it became a natural skill. The moment that an educator loses intellectual curiosity is the moment he or she starts falling behind. It doesn't come naturally to all of us, but we can't stand in the pulpit and preach lifelong learning if we don't belong to the church. An insatiable mind is always in the lead.

What's Next?

What's next is adding your name to the list of experts. The hope of this book, this journey, is that you will continue developing, continue growing, and continue doing the hardest job on the planet—effectively leading a school. That means creating a culture that "grows" the best kids, the kindest people, the most creative minds, and a warm place that reeks of safety, love, compassion, and caring. Become the leader that these highly accomplished folks have described. Make the world a better place.

A little kindness from person to person
is better than a vast love
for all humanity.

Richard Dehmel, poet/writer

Chapter 11

Take Care of Yourself Too!

This is a chapter about you, the principal. Not your unique qualities as a building leader, but you as a human being. Specifically it is about *your* wellness. It is near the end of the book because, as in real life, we often put ourselves last when it comes to our own welfare and health. Perhaps it should be first, but truthfully we are so concerned about doing the job as best we can, we often forget that we do our best work when we feel the best.

This chapter includes what works and what doesn't. It is divided into a variety of wellness categories. To get the most out of the following, think about your own lifestyle as a person and as the building leader. Consider whether some of the changes could truly be *life saving*.

I'm not an expert in psychology, exercise, or any of the six categories we are going to discuss, but I have done extensive research and I have lived through many of the situations you will read about. I do feel qualified to write this chapter because I am still kicking after a long life in this profession and I have learned tons of information from my peers and from the generous, and sometimes heartbreaking, stories they have shared. I have also survived seven school bond issues, one consolidation, dozens of boards, some wonderful coworkers, and several peers with situations that have caused me to do my homework so I could help them as their leader. We are in this together and at times our health and happiness are directly related to the well-being of those we work with, for, and, at times, against. Our job can cause us heartburn as well as heartache. It can (and will) cause stress and angst. It can also cause (and will) tears of joy along with tears of sorrow. It may put a strain on your relationships at home and school, and at times you will be forced to make decisions that will be hard on your mind and body. No one said being a principal was an easy job.

(If they did, you should wonder about them.) It is a tough job with lots of wear and tear on your body and spirit, but it can be a wonderful job at the same time. You need to be able to see both sides, handle both sides, survive both sides, and enjoy the goodness while fending off the negatives. I hope this chapter helps you do both.

For the rest of this chapter I am going to lead you through five categories of health, five different components that comprise your whole being. Each one interacts with the other, and all set the stage for success or failure.

I have shared the material in this chapter with many audiences, both in and out of the field of education. Personal wellness is not exclusive to our profession, but principals work under very stressful situations and have high demands on their time, abilities, and overall wellness. I can also tell you that many people have shared with me that the information you are about to read was meaningful, and in some cases, life changing. If this chapter is going to make you a better principal it must be owned and put into practice, and thus willpower and determination must be added to the mix.

If you decide to implement any changes in your lifestyle, think them through carefully. You may even want to discuss them with a professional. I remember a principal coming up to me at an academy I was giving. She said, "I don't think you will remember me. I attended a workshop you gave a year ago and the topic was wellness. Something you said stuck in my head, so I decided to implement a few of the suggestions concerning physical and professional health." She then took out a picture of herself taken about the time of the workshop the year before. I was shocked. She looked much older and very heavy. I looked at her more carefully. She had a new hairstyle, a more modern (and very professional) outfit, and her shoes went from the Dark Ages to what you would see on most well-dressed ladies today. She then told me she had lost over 100 pounds! She gave me all the credit, which I flipped immediately right back to her. I told her, in no uncertain terms, that I may have planted a seed, but she did all the gardening and was now reaping the benefits. I asked her what it was that stuck in her head. She replied, "You said that we have a great influence on the lives of many people as a school administrator, but that influence drops off dramatically if we drop dead on the job." She wasn't smiling. She said she needed a physical makeover and a professional upgrade. She accomplished both and seemed to be very confident and happy with her new look, new energy, and, she happily reported, with a new and better job. So, be prepared, you may be in for something that you don't expect from reading this chapter! Are a few life changes afoot?

You Are in Control

This is about *you* and the first thing we have to agree on is that *you* are in control! Each of us has direct control over the most important things in our lives. For instance, we can control what we eat, how we respond to stressful situations, our aerobic and strength-building options, our daily habits, and we can control *our half* of most relationships. We also control what we believe in—and we determine our own value systems.

As school administrators I would assume most of us are fairly, if not highly, intelligent. We know that we might die before the day is over and that there is no guarantee we won't get cancer, have a heart attack, or lose our marbles. On the other hand, we are all smart enough to know that we can turn the odds in our favor by following reasonable rules, accepting proven research, and living responsibly. As I said, there are no guarantees on our future, but can we agree that right now we do control making good or bad decisions about how we live?

When people watch or listen to you, what do they see? Do they see a principal who is energetic, healthy, and a positive role model? Do they someone who exemplifies self-control? Do they see someone who looks and acts professional? Do they see a person who they respect on the job as well as after hours? If so, they will more than likely follow your lead. Your wellness affects more than just you and your family, it sets the stage for others. You are a walking, talking role model of what you do, what you say, and what you profess.

The bottom line is that *you* are in control. The buck really does stop with *you* when it comes to personal decisions. Did you ever see anyone who was smoking have the tobacco forcibly stuffed down their throat? Did you ever see anyone force-fed that extra taco with hot sauce and a third beer? Did you ever see a principal who was superglued to their desk, preventing them from walking? Since YOU have the control, let's talk about taking charge and making a difference.

Ten Basics You Already Know

Here are some recommendations that I have gathered from popular health journals and medical organizations:

1. Exercise for 30 minutes a day.
Don't panic! Don't start to list all the excuses that everyone else makes, like no time, no equipment, too tired, or too weak. And don't say, "I'm active enough on the job!" You'll soon see that this may be one of the easiest of the recommendations to follow.

2. Don't use any type of tobacco product.
Can you read? If you can, then read carefully the side of the package that contains the cigar, cigarette, or chew. Tobacco kills. It doesn't take a nuclear scientist to know that tobacco complicates your body, your systems, your mind, and the impression you make on others. It makes you cough, stink, and get sick—then it contributes to an earlier death. Sure, there are smokers who live to be a hundred. There are also survivors who have jumped out of airplanes.

3. Don't drink alcohol.
But if you do, do it in moderation. My dad died from cirrhosis of the liver. He stopped drinking the last two years of his life. It was too late. It was a miserable way to lose a good guy. I also know two people who lost their lives because someone had a couple of beers, compromised their judgment, and ran their vehicle into theirs. Is a glass of wine bad for you? Will a couple of beers give you a disease? I don't think so. Can alcohol do

funny things to people who have high stress jobs, like *you*? Yep. Alcohol can be the fuse on a stick of dynamite. So why take the chance? Why risk your health or your reputation? Ever hear of a community member or coworker criticized for not drinking?

4. Eat a balanced diet.
A diet should include fruits, vegetables, and whole grains. Do you want to know just how easy this is to do? A glass of V8, an apple, and two helpings of vegetables (yes, even French fries count), and you have met "daily minimum requirements." Vary that a little and you are doing more than the minimum in most cases. I have a hard time finding any health list that doesn't give this recommendation top billing. Almost any culture that boasts good health also has a good diet. Why don't we?

5. Maintain a healthy weight.
This is really easier than you may think. You don't have to be a twig to be healthy. A healthy weight for you might even be a bit on the hefty side. Research is now saying that each individual has a unique "prime weight." The old charts listing a target weight for a certain height are disappearing. That is good news for most of us!

6. Spend time on relationships.
What? From fruits and exercise to being lovey-dovey? You bet. A happy home life is just as important to good health as are bananas and bike rides. A healthy family life reduces stress, promotes good digestion, minimizes diseases, and gives you a better attitude. Research also tells us that a person who kisses their spouse daily both morning and night lives 5.5 years longer than one who doesn't.

7. Be strong spiritually.
Spirituality covers a lot of options. It includes a sense of belonging, a trust in others, or a well-developed faith. They all add up to a longer life. Statistics tell us that married people live longer than unmarried people. And those who married in a church live even longer than those who didn't. The relation-

ship between spiritual wellness and physical wellness is heavily researched.

8. Challenge your mind every day.
This means reading, doing crossword puzzles, engaging in a topical discussion, playing cards, doing challenging games on your "Zoom" device, or creating something. It means keeping your mind challenged. Mental exercise is as important as physical exercise. I recently read that old people who play video games live longer than those who don't. I guess an Xbox is on my Christmas list!

9. Be proactive.
Get vaccines, flu shots, and take a multivitamin. When you have a cold, rest and drink fluids. When you are dizzy, sit down. If you experience unusual pains or pressures while under stress, see a doctor. Don't be afraid to seek help. A dead brave guy doesn't make a big impression.

10. Wear your seat belts.
Yes, this makes the top ten list most of the time because it does save lives. Wear your seat belts when you go to the grocery store or to another state. Before you turn the key, click your belt. And make sure everyone in the car does the same. Wear them on the plane, too. And if you don't know how to put them on, listen to the attendant.

This is a simple yet comprehensive list. Imagine if each of us worked hard to embrace these ten items regularly. Which ones can you check off right now because you have already made the commitment to do them? Go back and reread the list and see where you stand. Be honest. The more you can check off, the fewer you need to improve. Now think about an action plan for those that need your attention. How hard would that plan be to develop? Let's find out. Let's look at the five categories of health and consider a plan for each.

Physical Health

The first, and most obvious, is your physical health. Here is a simple plan to make a difference physically.

Conduct a self-assessment.

Get an unbiased and true picture of yourself. Weigh yourself. Tape measure yourself. Stand naked in front of a mirror. (Protect the neighbors and close the curtains first.) Look and take note how you measure up right now. Think about what you are and aren't able to do. Could you run around the block without getting out of breath or dropping over in the neighbor's bushes? Could you walk up four flights of stairs without stopping? Can you touch your toes without falling over? What can't you do now that you could do a year ago, five years ago, or when you were 16? When did you have your last physical? Do you need one before you start?

Develop a vision.

Picture your self as you would like others to see you. Don't plan on going from Oliver Hardy to Tom Cruise (or Melissa McCarthy to Julia Roberts) before your next paycheck. It won't happen. Be realistic. If you have bad teeth, get them fixed. If you need a new "do," then "do" it. If you need to update your wardrobe, go to the mall. If you need to build muscles and strength, make time to work out. Create a vision of what a principal should look like—then get there!

Set realistic goals.

If you need to lose 40 pounds, shoot for five. Then, when you reach that goal, set another. If you would like to stop smoking, picture your lungs pink and soft instead of black and crusty. If you want to regain some lost strength and be able to press 200 pounds again, set a goal of 50 right now. You can always up it later. If you can't curl 25 pounds, start with five. Don't fret about where you start, just look forward to where you will be going.

Implement your plan.

Making a plan is easy. Not following it is even easier. The result is obvious: you are still in the same shape as before, but now you also have a load of guilt to carry around along with your extra tonnage. Avoid all this and follow your plan! If you find it was too aggressive, modify it. Remember that some progress is better than no progress. Let me state that again because it is the key to improvement. *Some progress is better than no progress!* If you set a goal to walk two miles every day and at the end of the first week you only walked a total of five miles, that is five miles better than the week before! Restate your goals and make improvements. Once you see results you will want to do more. Let me repeat that too: *Once you see results, you will want to do more!*

Evaluate your plan.

Give yourself one month of sticktoitiveness before you evaluate. If after a month of real dedication you don't see any improvement, then (1) kick the plan up a notch, (2) rewrite the plan from scratch, or (3) give it another month. *Just don't quit!*

Don't make it so difficult.

To lose weight you must eat less and exercise more. There, that saves you $89.99 for that weight loss program you were thinking about buying. You don't need that $1,500 home gym either, or the one on TV for four payments of $39.99 each. A few bucks for dumbbells at Walmart, a space on the floor, and a TV set to watch while you pound the iron will work just fine. Exercise and watch TV. A treadmill is even easier to use. You can get a used one really cheap from someone who didn't follow through on their own plan.

Here's a Free Physical Wellness Plan!

I bet when you bought this book you didn't think you were going to get a free, personalized physical wellness plan! If you use it, you will probably improve both how you feel and how effective you are as a principal.

Has it been a while since you exercised? Do you pant after a flight of stairs? Have you added 10, 20, 50, 80, or more pounds since you were at your best weight? Do you find yourself a bit sluggish at certain times during the day, and maybe a bit less patient than you used to be? If you answered yes to any of these questions then I suggest you get a routine physical before you start any plan of action. (You should do this anyway at least once every other year, and don't forget those recommended female and male tests on a regular basis.) Do you have a family history of heart or lung disease, cancer, or other illnesses? If so, get an annual exam. Catch them early and you can beat almost anything these days. Now's the time to stop reading about it and make an appointment. Go ahead, I'll wait. Oh yes, one more thing, have those moles and oddities on your skin been looked at, even if they aren't bothering you?

Excuse me, did you make that appointment?

Let's start with the fundamentals of weight. You don't need a book for this because it is really simple. Fat and muscle add weight to your body. To lose weight you have to lose fat or muscle. You lose weight by burning calories. You gain weight by consuming more calories than you burn. The math is straightforward. Lose more calories than you consume and you lose weight. You are burning calories as you read this book, when you sit at the computer, when you sleep, when you watch a movie, when you sit on a bench and look at the sunset... as long as you're not eating at the same time. You can even drink a nice *cold* glass of water when you do all of these things and lose additional calories because water doesn't have any calories to start with. Even better, you burn calories heating up your body after the *cold* water cooled it down. If you didn't consume any food in a day and just sat around and watched TV, read the paper, or played solitaire, you'd lose weight. Duh. But you might pack it back on the next day when your appetite kicked in.

So here is my theory after years of reading and study. I call it the "Two-A-Month Plan." Take two pounds off your weight each month until your goal is reached. That's 24 pounds in a year. Kick it up a notch and it can easily be a "Three-A-Month

Plan." It takes a change in your life habits once it begins to work and you get into it big time. You need one thing before you start—a steady weight level. If your weight has not fluctuated more than 2-3 pounds in the last three months, on the average, you have a steady weight. If you have picked up five or more pounds, you will have to modify this plan. If you are already purposefully losing weight, this plan will help the process.

Are you ready? Here it is: lose (or don't add) about 200 calories a day. That's it. There are lots of ways to do it. I recommend a combination of *burning calories* (action) and *reducing intake* (less food). Now here is why I think this plan is doable and can easily fit the principal's lifestyle: it takes almost no effort to accomplish.

1. If you drink one can of regular soda each day, just switch to diet and you just saved about 150 calories.
2. Do you eat a candy bar each day? Eat half of one and you just saved 100 calories.
3. Do you eat a doughnut in the morning? Eat half of one, or cut it out altogether, or replace it with something lower in calories.
4. Do you drink a big glass of orange juice? Drink eight ounces and save about 100 calories.
5. One pat of butter is 84 calories.
6. Order a medium-size bag of fries instead of the large one at McDonald's and you just saved over 300 calories, and you can save 300 more if you eat a regular hamburger instead of a Big Mac.
7. You want to know the easiest way to cut 200 or more calories a day? Sit down at any meal and eat only three-quarters of what is put in front of you.
8. If you usually pour on a healthy dose of salad dressing, pour three-quarters of that dose. Or replace regular salad dressing with no-fat dressing, or just vinegar and oil, and you have cut out a load of calories and fat!
9. If you eat pizza, put a paper towel on top of the pizza for ten seconds and you will reduce the calories by an average of 17% just by not eating the fat you take off the top! Put sal-

sa or barbecue sauce on your baked potato instead of butter or sour cream and you just eliminated a huge amount of calories and you might find the end product even tastier!

Isn't that easy? Eat less, but do *it reasonably and regularly.* Bypass one treat a day and you will easily meet your goal. But remember two things: (1) you have to do this every day, and (2) it has to be based on a stable diet. Meaning that you can't add anything to your normal eating patterns.

One more thing, and it this is important: There are lots of theories about weight loss. Some say you need to burn rather than reduce calories. Some say how you do it will affect fat and or muscle loss. Some say not to count calories, just change your eating mentality. Listen to anyone you want but it boils down to this: Take in less, and you lose weight. Burn off more, and you lose weight. Do it for two days and quit, and you won't lose weight in the long run. Do it for 90 days, consistently and with purpose, and you will lose weight and have a higher probability of keeping it off.

I didn't forget the exercise part. If you want, start walking each night for thirty minutes. You can burn about 150 calories in a nice, easy, thirty-minute stroll. You can also burn 50 calories if you walk an extra ten minutes during the day. You can even do this on company time and be paid for it! The next time you have a message to deliver, walk across the office, go to the next building, climb the stairs, do anything as long as you move. If you move ten minutes more than usual each day, you chalk up 50 calories on your road to better health. Wash a normal load of dishes rather than use the dishwasher: 94 calories burned. Ride your bike slowly and on flat land for only 15 minutes and you chopped 110 calories. Drink water and you burn no calories, but you don't gain any either. I told you this was easy. Drink ice water and you burn 15 calories for each 12 ounces.

Summary

Drink one less beer or one less Pepsi or eat one handful less of snacks each day, and do about 15 minutes of easy (no sweat) exercise and you will, without a doubt, lose 5-10 pounds or more in the next three months (as long as everything else in your diet or activity is stable). You will most likely keep it off too since you have developed both an awareness of healthy habits, and the ability to put them into action.

That's it. Want to learn lots more? Go to Nutrition.gov. You can also get helpful information from the website of your favorite fast food place about what foods are best to eat, and what to avoid. Remember, a negative 200-calorie shift a day equals about two pounds of weight loss a month as long as everything else remains neutral.

This Is NEAT

Here is something else to consider. Most people think that exercise burns most of our calories. Not even close. Every day 60-70% of all the calories are burned at a constant simmer. Those are the calories that stoke the furnace of automated processes that keep us alive. It's called "basal metabolism." For men it requires about 11 calories a pound a day. A 200-pound person would need about 2,200 calories just to function. Add to the basal metabolism two other types of burned calories, those you burn in exercise activities such as walking, running, swimming, weight lifting, canoeing, at the gym, etc., and those you burn during **N**on-**E**xercise **A**ctivity **T**hermogenesis, or NEAT. Those are calories we burn for everything except sleeping, eating, or gym/sports exercise. If you up the NEAT calories you will increase your calorie burn substantially.

Here are four more ways to burn calories with NEAT, according to http://www.neatweightloss.com:

Burn more calories at the office.
Having a sedentary job isn't a direct cause of obesity, but sitting for extended periods could become a cause of weight gain

in some people. The American Heart Association reported that "obese individuals appear to exhibit an innate tendency to be seated for 2.5 hours per day more than sedentary lean counterparts." Researchers estimated that if obese individuals could adopt the NEAT habits of their lean counterparts, they could burn an additional 350 calories per day. If you have a desk job, create a habit of getting up for at least 15 minutes every hour. Take a walk to the farthest restroom or water cooler, run an errand, take the stairs instead of the elevator, or do your filing from a standing rather than sitting position. Grab a few co-workers and make increasing your NEAT part of a healthy-office routine. Principals should be visible anyway, so avoid being a fixture in the office.

Burn more calories while you relax.
How many hours will you spend in front of the television tonight? You can burn extra calories by simply adding some light activity to your TV viewing and relaxation time. Fold laundry, dust furniture, or sweep the floor while you watch television. Not only will the activity boost your caloric expenditure, but you will eat less in front of the television if your hands are busy. You can even burn calories during other leisure activities. If you like to talk on the phone, walk around during your chat instead of sitting down. And try to limit entertainment-related computer time to 15-minute intervals.

Burn more calories with daily chores.
According to the activity tracker at *CalorieCount.com*, household or routine office chores can burn a few hundred calories per hour. The actual number depends on your size and gender. For example, a petite woman burns about 160 calories per hour doing moderate chores while a larger man would burn substantially more. But who would have thought that sweeping your floor could cause weight loss? Grab a mop and do a complete housecleaning workout to burn calories and tidy up at the same time. Once the cleaning is done, there are always organizational tasks that can help you improve your energy balance. Organize your closet, unpack boxes, or clean the office to increase your NEAT.

Burn more calories at social events.
How many times have you entered a party in a friend's home and scanned the room for a comfy place to sit? The next time you go to a party, burn extra calories by becoming more social. Stand or circle the room and talk to as many partygoers as possible. Offer to help in the kitchen, take a tour of the garden, or greet guests at the door to stay active. You'll be the life of the party and increase your NEAT at the same time.

Mental Wellness

Now that you have worked on your diet and exercise, let's check your mental wellness. If you are a typical administrator you can spell stress at least 30 different ways. If you experience aches or pains only when you are under stress, see a doctor. Don't think twice. Do it. No fooling, this is important. Don't die thinking about it. Stress absolutely does cause physical problems, and sometimes delay is fatal. If your stress is occasional and doesn't cause you to turn blue, why not set some time aside each day for yourself? How about taking 15 minutes in the morning for *you*? Do things you enjoy like reading, writing, surfing Facebook, playing the piano, or walking. Another thing is to schedule regular family time, like a weekly date with your spouse or a commitment to watch your kid's activities.

You can reduce stress by reducing time wasters. Organize your day better. Learn to control the phone, your Zoom devices, email, and other distractions. Delegate more.

We have mentioned this before, but it is worth repeating: Take a nap when you need one. When you can't keep your eyes open, or just need to escape the pressure, close your door, turn off the lights, and nap. You will be more productive, do a better job, and give the school higher quality work after a short nap. If you are worried about what your boss will think, try to remember that *you* are the boss! Take a nap if you need one—or take a walk. Depressurize yourself by getting away for 10 minutes. Don't forget to come back. Or call a friend, your spouse, or the operator when you need to talk to someone.

Sometimes to get over a problem all we need to do is share it with someone else. Learn to be a talker when you need to.

Here's another idea: keep your office and your desk orderly. It helps keep your mind in order. And don't whine, don't moan, and don't gripe about your stressful job; instead, spend that energy making changes. If hearing whiners is stressful, don't be one.

Mental wellness can be complicated. If you experience longer than normal bouts of confusion or depression, if you find yourself angry for no reason, if you find yourself turning a minor incident into a national calamity, if you discover that a lot of things really bother you all of a sudden, if you have a serious urge to do something harmful to yourself or others, if you think of leaving your job or home to escape your situation, or if you don't care about your family or work and don't know why, these are all indicators that you need to find someone to talk to. Employee Assistance Programs help. A minister, priest, rabbi, or some clerical person can help. Your medical doctor can help. The key word is HELP. Get some. You are a talented, educated, proven leader. You are also human and work in a tough profession. All of us are challenged to keep things in order, to balance our responsibilities, and make life work. Getting help is not a sign of weakness, it's a sign of strength.

Social Wellness: The Art of Good Relationships

Your social wellness is very important. Studies tell us that the six most frequent problems in this area deal with in-laws, money, housework, sex, stress, and parenthood. No principal is immune to these issues. So how do we come up with a quick solution to maintaining social wellness? Experts say maintaining better communications, sharing the workload at home, trusting each other, getting outside help, accepting relationships, and adapting to change are key solutions. "Easy for you to say!" you say. You could write a book on this topic, in fact many have, so why not read one and learn how to improve relationship skills? Learn the importance of treating your spouse better than you treat your coworkers. (Who hasn't come home cranky but was great to everyone at work?) Learn that it is more important to watch your kids play ball than going to some meetings. Learn the need to have something to do away from work such as singing in a choir, going to movies, playing cards, golfing, doing yard work for your in-laws. (Who said all my ideas are good ones?)

There are a few tips that you may want to consider when it comes to social wellness. First, get your priorities in line. What *is* most important to you? Is it the job or your spouse? Is it family or income? Is it your spiritual beliefs or your social life? Is it a beer with the guys, volleyball with the girls, cards on Friday night, watching the kids play baseball, spending Sundays with the family, never missing church, or being at school for every athletic event? You make the choice because these are things in your life that you control. Make a decision to "date" your spouse one night a week and you may save a marriage. Talk about sexual needs openly and you may improve your relationship by one letter grade or more. Set your priorities so they fit with those of your family, friends, support systems, and employer and you are one step closer to good social health and wellness.

Easy? No way. This one takes planning and commitment. Work on your half of the relationships and see what happens. You might also go back to Chapter 1 and reread "The Right to Have a Life" and "The Right to Seek Help."

Spiritual Wellness

I've been in education, in the United States, long enough to know what you are probably thinking, "tread lightly here." This is a personal zone and we are all well programmed to take baby steps around religion and school issues.

If you don't think spiritual wellness is important, skip this section. No one will know except you and that all-knowing spiritual being that you may or may not believe in or even think is real. Go ahead, move on if you want—another choice.

If you are reading this paragraph you are still here. Good. Personally, I don't see how any administrators could feel that they have done anything without the minute-by-minute help of some higher power. If you have a faith don't be afraid to share it. Wellness comes from honest communication. Don't impose your faith on others, but never feel you need to hide it or avoid it. God is not a dirty word. Nor is Jesus, Buddha, Islam, LDS, synagogue, or the pope. Spirituality is a personal thing, but having it, sharing it, using it, living by it, and reflecting it doesn't need to be. It is who you are. If you are comfortable with spiritual beliefs then you are on the way to real, personal wellness.

Study after study tells us that staying connected spiritually promotes extended longevity, fewer health problems, and greater satisfaction with life. It also boosts immunity levels, promotes better health habits, improves mental stability, and slows memory loss. These aren't opinions, they are the results of numerous scientific studies. Again, the choice is yours.

Professional Health

Often forgotten and seldom discussed is our "professional health." I define professional health simply as how you behave, look, and grow in your profession.

Don't you feel better when you are satisfied about how you look? Dress is a very important part of your professional image and health. Attention to style and trends are important. Improvements in dress and grooming are easy. Look at others you respect, then look at yourself. Is it time for a tune-up? Or maybe it's time for a complete overhaul? Then do it. If in doubt, go to a store that has a suit or dress department with people who cater to professionals and ask for their advice. Skip the farm equipment stores.

Want a few tips in this area? Pick up a copy of any popular style magazine or hit the Internet and search for grooming tips. Maybe it's time you are reminded that your tie should come down to a point about one inch below the top of your belt when you are standing up, not six inches short of your belt, or so long you can zip the end in your fly. Maybe it's time you sat down at the mall and looked at what people are wearing on their feet. If 90% of the women wear shoes that show their toes, maybe it is time to box up those dress combat boots. Are you still wearing a size 34 waist pair of pants but the length has gone from 34 to 30? It may be because you are wearing it below your tire rather than around your waist. (Go back and read the part about physical wellness.) Has that hairdo been the same for 15 years? I wonder how a new one might look.

One more thought. Find a friend or friends you trust and admire. Tell them you want a professional-look redo (don't ask them if you need one). Tell them you admire how they look professionally. Ask for advice. They will be complimented and helpful. Make no promises that you will implement their suggestions, and tell them you are asking a few other people too to help you gather choices, thus, if you don't like something they say they will not be offended if you show up in a month still looking like the left-hand picture in a makeover article.

Are you professionally bored? It happens to every school administrator at times. The answer is simple, but not always easy to alter. Make yourself change your routine. Change your job description (give yourself some different responsibilities). Change your job (move). Or maybe all you need to do is change your attitude.

Professional wellness is more important than just looks and attitude. It defines you. The results? Others may start describing you in terms like classy, sophisticated, sharp, motivating, the best, a mentor, always on top of things, knowledgeable, willing to help.

And Finally...

As a principal you are responsible for so many lives and so many jobs that you owe it to them to be the best you can be. But you owe it to yourself and those you love to be healthy as well as happy. Your physical, mental, social, spiritual, and professional wellness should not take a back seat to anything. *Now* is the time to evaluate where you are and where you want to be. *Now* is the time to begin a plan. Any improvement you make today is a start. It may be just enough to get you going on a program that not only makes you a better administrator but also a happier and better person.

YOU are important. Take care of yourself too!

The School Principal's Toolbook

Chapter 12

Tools and Thoughts for the Principal

All of the previous chapters in this toolbook have addressed specific topics. This one touches on many. I'm hoping, after you read this final chapter, that you will add to your list of tools some tricks of the trade, and words of inspiration to put these tricks into action.

When you spend years and years collecting data, reading books, listening to great educators, and work side by side with exceptional administrators, you collect a plethora of outstanding material. Much of it can't be compartmentalized into chapters. Some ideas stand by themselves, are more suited for a paragraph, or are simply single sentences that might move or inspire. Educators have a unique habit, we like to share good ideas, and that is what this chapter is all about, sharing.

Dr. Fred Singleton, one of my expert contributors, and a longtime partner in administrative collaboration, wrote the following: "I am not sure a book can make a great principal. It can improve one's performance and give the individual some ideas, but in my opinion, a quality principal comes to the job with these qualities: compassion, desire, ethics, honesty, and has a strong desire to make changes to improve opportunities. Being an effective principal cannot be implanted by attending a few workshops or reading a book."

This book is not intended, by itself, to make anyone a great, super-achieving school administrator. It is, however, intended to spark the imagination, refuel depleted cisterns of creativity, inspire action, and give principals—rookie to retirement—something to ponder. It is intended to be one of many resources that collectively push the reader to a new place. If this book pushes you one inch closer to denting the universe in a significant way, or even in a modest way, I will be pleased. No, I will be ecstatic.

The School Principal's Toolbook

I hope that in the previous chapters you have been challenged and maybe even validated.

This chapter is designed to do the same. There is no order to the entries you are about to read.

Although some of the names of the sources have faded over the years, I have tried to give credit where I can. If the source is unknown, I signed it that way. The rest are gifts from me.

Enjoy.

*****

Wherever you go, go with all your heart.

Confucius

*****

Everyone needs to be motivated, including you. Buy, download, or find some of the many motivational tapes, podcasts, or CD's that are available. Or better yet, let the district buy them and put them into your school's professional library when you are done. Listen to them in your car on the way to work or a meeting. Even five minutes of a good speaker can get your heart moving and push you forward. Tapes for businesspeople, including salespersons, are good too. An old favorite whose message is timeless is Zig Ziglar.

*****

The hopes of the world rest on the flexibility, vigor, capacity for new thought, and the fresh outlook of the young.

Dwight D. Eisenhower

*****

Never forget to tap the minds of your newest and youngest team members. They can teach you "Zoom" better than anyone because many have grown up with it. They also have ideas and impressions that you may never have thought of. When you do brainstorming, have a mix of young, middle-aged, and old coots—and learn from each.

*****

If you ever need a helping hand, you'll find one at the end of your arm.

Yiddish proverb

*****

Do you love your spouse and family? Then why, at the end of a busy and stress-filled day, do you give them grief? (Admit it, you don't always treat them as politely as you treat those at work.) Remind yourself, before you walk into the house, that the people inside it love you, and they deserve *your* love, not your grief. Put a little label on the outside door that simple says "PILY." This will remind you that "People Inside Love You"—then dump your troubles, pressures, and stress outside. Don't take them in with you!

*****

Sometimes only a change of viewpoint is needed to convert a tiresome duty into an interesting opportunity.

Alberta Flanders

*****

An assistant principal, who was responsible for first-hour late arrivals, and issues related to attendance, once told me that the job became routine and burdensome. So he decided to focus on one student at a time, going beyond the required procedures. He would put the name of this student on his desk and do extended homework on why he/she was tardy, or what the real causes were for being absent. And, student-by-student, he made a difference and solved many problems that would have slipped though the cracks. It gave him an entirely different outlook on this "task." And, there was always an index card on his desk with the name of the student he hoped to change for the better.

*****

Get wired. Utilize technology to make your life and your job easier. If you don't know how, take some classes. Many are offered online, are short, and are easy to do. There are literally thousands of time-saving apps that you can use to help manage time. Don't type when you can use voice recognition. Check out Evernote, one of the most popular lines of time-management products available. Ask people what they use and why.

*****

"6 Common Mistakes that Undermine Motivation" is an article from a recent *Kappan Magazine*. If you are trying to motivate your team, or students, these are mistakes frequently made: (1) Don't tell students they are studying something "because you have to." Instead give them a defined purpose for engagement. (2) Don't dismiss a topic with a comment like "Sorry, folks, it's math," give them something more. (3) It doesn't help to tell adolescents, "When you grow up." This is hurtful, not helpful. (4) "Architects use geometry" is something that may alienate the majority. (5) "You need to know this for college" is lame. Find a more immediate, intrinsic interest. And realize some have no intention of going to college. (6) "Let's play a game" does not align the content to relevance. These same concepts can be applied to the administrator working with the staff. Make your efforts to motivate relevant to their position and the goals they hopefully own.

*****

It's been my experience that true burnout doesn't come from too much activity. Burnout comes from unmet expectations.

Kelly Clark

The School Principal's Toolbook

*****

When people know you truly care, they are willing to forget all the negative things they were thinking about you. In fact, they will.

Terry Bell

******

If your building or district doesn't have a partnership with the area businesses, then start one. It can be a wonderful resource for all sorts of things. It makes great relationships in your community. If you have no idea how to start one then just ask around. Many schools have business-education partnerships that just might serve as a model. Or search "business education partnerships." If you lament the fact that your little town doesn't have businesses to partner with, remember that even the gas station, tavern, or feed mill work with, or distribute products for, huge corporations that probably have education divisions eager to help local schools.

*****

Three words that can help form a successful mindset: Relate-Elate-Celebrate. When you form a bond with team members you relate. When you affirm their goals and recognize their efforts, you elate. When they succeed, you celebrate. Put them together and you move mountains.

*****

Live like a goose. They work together, follow their designated leader faithfully, take turns doing the hard jobs, honk at each other (but only sounds of encouragement), and stand by each other in times of distress or need. As they spend time working toward accomplishing their goals, their collective actions actually provide a lifting power that supports and motivates each member of the team.

There is a great video on this topic. Search YouTube for "Wisdom of Geese." This a good video to share at a faculty meeting.

*****

I received this letter from a former teacher, now a school principal.

Dear Jim,

Today is our last day of school before our Christmas break and I was remembering fondly how you would travel to each classroom in the district to say thanks to all of the staff members. I remember first meeting you on such a December day when I was a long-term sub in the district. It made me feel great that you would take a couple of minutes to pop your head in every classroom to say thank you and Happy Holidays. It was the first time we had ever met, and it left a very positive memory.

I know you treated everyone with kindness and respect, but it certainly was meaningful to me and influenced how I work with my staff, students, and parents.

Thankful thoughts from Wisconsin,

Curt

[As a principal (and later as a superintendent) I did this faithfully every year, visiting every classroom and all noncertified staff, wishing every team member and student Happy Holidays and thanking every staff member for their service. It was the best day of the year for me. It was also exhausting, covering every classroom in eight buildings, five towns, and including all members of the team. *But I loved it.*]

*****

The School Principal's Toolbook

Thank-you letters, even years later, make a huge difference. Why not write one today?

*****

Better to ask twice than to lose your way once.

Danish proverb

*****

Teachers shouldn't punish everyone when they can't find the criminal. Suspending or keeping an entire group after school because you can't determine who is at fault is not right. It is better to narrow down the possible suspects, and then call their parents and ask for help in determining who is guilty. Parental pressure often gives the results you are looking for.

The same is true for principals—changing rules or expectations for the entire group because one or two team members don't follow them; it's simply not right. Find the culprit, deal with them privately, reset your expectations of professional behavior, and celebrate the fact that most of the team is already doing what is right.

*****

The greatest thing you will ever give to the world is your commitment to leave what you find in better condition than the way you found it. Leave a single light in a place where there was once darkness so those coming behind you may see further and begin where you left off.

Tonny K. Brown

*****

There are many resources that will help you become a better leader. One of my favorites is the book *Developing the Leader*

Within You by John C. Maxwell. Just a list of the chapters makes you think. Maxwell has greatly influenced me over the years.

Chapters:

1. The definition of leadership: Influence
2. The key to leadership: Priorities
3. The most important ingredient of leadership: Integrity
4. The ultimate test of leadership: Creating Positive Change
5. The quickest way to gain leadership: Problem-Solving
6. The extra plus in leadership: Attitude
7. Developing your most appreciable asset: People
8. The indispensable quality of leadership: Vision
9. The price tag of leadership: Self-Discipline
10. The most important lesson of leadership: Staff Development

*****

If you confiscate a cell phone or tablet, be wary of looking at or searching any of the data. You may come across more than you want to know. In the legal academies I present with a nationally known school attorney we strongly recommend that you make sure all Zoom devices are turned off and powered down when you collect them, then have a police officer or resource officer do the search of content on the device. This protects you as much as them. If you find something inappropriate, such as sexting, you can be considered looking at pornography. Don't risk it. If you doubt this advice, talk to a school attorney.

*****

One way to get high blood pressure is to go mountain climbing over molehills.

Earl Wilson

*****

The School Principal's Toolbook

Follow up on discipline immediately. If calling parents is required, do it as soon as possible. Call parents before Johnny gets home from school and gives his one-sided version. Avoid calling only when it is convenient for them. They might not like a call at work, for instance, but did you like the problem in the first place? One big warning: never call anyone until you have all the facts and know what you are talking about. You are the principal and they expect you to have the information correct.

*****

Take into account that great love and great achievements involve great risk.

Dalai Lama

*****

Although I use "notes" on my Zoom devices, and a handful of other organizers, I still like the old, hands-on, post-a-note method of organizing my list of things to do. I learned this from a principal at a workshop. She said she uses three different colored post-a-note pads. On the yellow ones she writes down her daily list of things to do, one per note. On the green ones are her tasks that she wants to complete in the next few days, and on the blue ones are her long-term tasks, and she adds notes of progress, with a date as she works toward completion of this goal, sometimes tacking on a second note when needed. She keeps all of these in one manila folder on her desk. She updates—adding, removing, and making notes at least two times per day. It works for her and it works for me, too.

*****

Except in situations of self-defense or prevention of injury, never hit, shove, push, or hurt anyone. You might want to, but don't. The minute you do, *you* might become the issue, and in today's climate, you might lose.

*****

The School Principal's Toolbook

I've learned that just one person saying to me, "You've made my day!" makes my day.

Andy Rooney

*****

Don't let a single day go by that you don't find someone to whom you can say, "You've made my day."

*****

Never lose control when disciplining. That's not always easy, but extremely important. Cool heads need to prevail. Keep cool. If necessary, have all the participants separated, then take a minute or two to collect your thoughts. This is true when dealing with kids, parents, teachers, irate citizens, or really anyone.

*****

If wisdom's ways you wisely seek, Five things observe with care, to whom you speak, of whom you speak, and how, and when, and where.

Laura Ingalls Wilder

*****

Three Things I Teach My Children

Be nice. It's easier to deal with people and things when you are pleasant.
Be smart. Be aware of your surroundings, and try to act with reason and intent.
Be safe. Life is fragile, and a moment's inattention can take it away.

Mike Gladys

*****

Never lie to a team member, a student, or anyone. It can haunt you forever, and it should.

*****

Recently a friend of mine related a story. He said he was in an office waiting in line to get to the service counter to trade in a cable box. The small office was crowded with people and two men were lamenting about their jobs. They were both school bus drivers and one was complaining about how terrible kids are today! They went back and forth how they both didn't like kids. The one driver said, "I have five more weeks of driving before I can retire, and I'm sure not looking forward to going back!" (The conversation took place during summer vacation.)

My friend, in his forties and father of three school-age kids, turned around to the guy and said, "Then don't go back. With that attitude you shouldn't be working for the school system or even around kids. And, I imagine, if you think about it, most kids are just fine. Maybe it isn't the kids, either, maybe it's you or your attitude."

He said the man melted and the room looked shocked that he had the fortitude to say what he said, but they also looked grateful. I know when he told me this story, I was not only grateful, but proud to consider him a friend.

No one should be employed by a school system if they don't love kids. No one.

*****

How is your office? Is it arranged in such as way that you encourage the casual passerby to feel a need to stop in for no reason at all? *You don't need those time eaters.* Arrange your desk so that you don't look out into the main office or hallway, so casual face contact is *avoided*. You can have an open-door policy without an arrangement that makes it easy for anyone to stop in and take up time with no reason for the visit.

The School Principal's Toolbook

*****

Learn what motivates the best. This is true for staff as well as students.

*****

Intrinsic motivation comes from a child's internal desire to complete a task because it's satisfying or pleasurable. Extrinsic motivation, however, drives a child to complete a task with the promise of outside rewards such as money or grades. Students continue to be motivated both by an internal drive for success as well as by external rewards. But, students who find internal motivation to engage their learning tend to have the most lasting success.

Lindsey Hill, *District Administrator Magazine*

*****

Life is tough, but you are tougher. This is especially true if you are an administrator.

James Francis

*****

Don't let a little dispute injure a great relationship.

Dalai Lama

The Dalai Lama's statement is particularly true when dealing with your team. One small incident, one hurtful comment, one unintentional misstep can fester and cause great divides. Fix problems immediately, and if you don't know what the problem is, ask. Tell whomever it is that your relationship is too important to be compromised. Fix it ASAP.

*****

Never laugh at anyone's dreams. People who don't have dreams don't have much.

*****

Do you want to encourage your teachers to eat lunch with their students? Offer them a free school lunch once a week if they eat at a student table. Set this up so all they need to do is tell the cashier. Some will take you up on the idea once in a while, some will do it regularly, and some only for special events. No matter what, it won't break the bank and you will reap many benefits.

*****

What is noble can be said in any language, and what is mean should be said in none.

Moses Ben Maimon

*****

Invite a group of senior citizens to tour your school and treat them to a school lunch. Allow time for Q/A. They will love it and you! Other ideas are to invites special groups like real estate agents, bankers, fast food managers, etc. The list is endless and the PR is wonderful.

*****

Never regret. If it's good, it's wonderful. If it's bad, it's experience.

Victoria Holt

*****

("SmartBrief was mentioned earlier but here are more details that may help you discover this amazing source of helpful information.)

Go to this website: SmartBrief.com. When you get there, click on "Browse Topics." Next click on "Education." Now click on the various topics for a list of extremely helpful articles, all in newsletter formats. These newsletters come regularly via email and contain summaries of current literature and research on a multitude of subjects—leadership, technology, teaching, etc. Once you select one, you will see that several resources show up, each with a sentence or two. Click on the topic and it takes you to the source. I bet you will be addicted to this resource and will learn a great deal about a great deal. I specifically enjoy the "nbpts Smartbrief" under Educational Leadership; this focuses on educational topics by nationally certified teachers. There is *no cost*, and you are not harassed with unrelated emails. Subscribe to this service, or to several, and you will be thankful for this resource! It is one of my favorites. No, it *is* my favorite.

*****

I've learned that the less time I have to work with, the more things I get done.

Andy Rooney

Isn't that the case with most principals? Little time, lots to do, and still very productive!

*****

Do you have a problem? Are you drinking too much, addicted to computer sites, interested and acting inappropriately with staff members, smoking pot, or have gambling issues? Are you mean or violent to your spouse or kids, do you steal, do you falsify reports or have a problem with honesty? Or are you struggling with something I haven't mentioned? Get help. Go to a private source and seek assistance. You are responsible for kids and your behavior needs to be addressed. Don't deny your needs, deal with them. Really. This is not a request, this is me begging you to take action. Your job is too important, so is your family, and so are you. Stop right now and think about it.

The School Principal's Toolbook

*****

Is your office homey or homely? My wife suggested two things, several years ago, to add to my man-office as she called it. She said, "You need to add a couple of big plants and put family pictures on that one table." I did both and it made a huge difference. I eventually exchanged the live plants for really nice-looking fake ones. I think I killed the real ones by watering them with half cans of Mountain Dew. The photos were great conversation openers with visitors. Mostly it made my office look more welcoming and tempered my positive attitude posters.

*****

Have a box of tissues handy in your office. Lots of people get emotional talking about their kids. But a candy dish is not a good idea unless you want people stopping by for no special reason other than getting a candy fix.

*****

There are many characteristics of leaders. For many years I asked my audiences to give me the top qualities that excellent leaders need to posses. I kept track of the list and then one day I read a small, but powerful book by John Maxwell on leadership. It is called *The 21 Indispensable Qualities of a Leader*. I compared my tally with Maxwell's, and my list had all of his, but two. His book not only lists them, it gives you instructions on attaining them. I have recommended this book to aspiring school leaders for years, and to leaders who want to perform a tune-up from the neck up. It is an excellent resource. I recommend reading one quality a day for a month, and then repeating the process for a full year. You will not only know them, you will begin to live them.

*****

When you walk through the halls inspecting your building, or just on a stroll, remember to look up. Custodians, principals,

The School Principal's Toolbook

teachers, etc., have a tendency to look ahead or down and often miss problems on the walls or ceilings. Learn to look for areas that need attention, take notes, *then see to it that things are corrected.*

*****

Use your cell phone to record things as you see them. School attorneys say "document, document, document" all the time. So if you see an incident, or need to react to a problem, pull out your phone, and then activate the app you use for notes. Use the voice recognition system to document, time, place, situation, and names. Keep updating the page throughout the issue and you will have an easy to print report. Also, use your phone to record things to celebrate, or to take photos of kids or team members doing neat things, or to help you stay organized. I've used my phone to take pictures of parents and their kids at concerts, games, etc., and then emailed them the photos. You earn lots of points for doing this!

*****

Everything counts! Everything you do helps or hurts, adds up or takes away.

Brian Tracy

*****

As soon as you see it, remove graffiti or fix vandalism. Repair broken windows or bent lockers immediately. Set this example and don't let anyone take pleasure in seeing the results of their mischief. It also follows the theory that if you handle small problems immediately, it curtails bigger ones from happening. An old Chinese proverb puts it this way: *A small hole not mended in time will become a big hole much more difficult to mend.*

*****

When I took over as principal in my first district there was a long history of kids soaping and waxing the school windows on Halloween night, sometimes with inappropriate words or comments. Trying to determine which group did it was not worth the effort. So I set my alarm for 3 a.m. the morning after Halloween, and armed with buckets of hot water, long scrub brushes, a paint bucket of gasoline, and a car washing mitt, I washed off the wax (with the gas), and scrubbed off the soap. The windows were not spotless in the morning, but no one could see the kids' handiwork. I told no one that I did it. No one. Not a word was said. The next year I set my alarm again to do the same thing, but to my surprise there was no wax or soap to be washed, and it never happened again. Amazing.

*****

The mediocre teacher tells.
The good teacher explains.
The superior teacher demonstrates.
The great teacher inspires.

William Arthur Ward

Substitute "administrator" for "teacher" and it still holds true. And remember that when you inspire one teacher they in turn may inspire thousands of students during their career.

*****

Evaluate, in depth, only the teachers that need it. Don't waste a lot of time on the top-rated excellent teachers, and don't waste time on those watching the clock waiting for the big hand to hit retirement. Spend most of your time with the new, the trying but struggling, those beginning to burn out, the ones that need a boost, or average-to-above average teachers, all of whom can improve. Find other ways to deal with the exceptional teachers rather than spending time doing evaluations, like having them mentor or share with others what makes them so successful.

*****

The School Principal's Toolbook

"Somehow I can't believe there are many heights that can't be scaled by a man who knows the secret of making dreams come true. This special secret, it seems to me, can be summarized in four C's. They are Curiosity, Confidence, Courage, and Constancy, and the greatest of these is Confidence. When you believe a thing, believe it all over, implicitly and unquestioning."

Walt Disney

*****

Bring an extra pair of Nikes and leave them in your closet. When the mood hits you, go outside and skip rope, throw a football, swing on the swings (you old swinger, you), and play. Or take a walk. If you want to pretend you are Mr. (or Ms) Rogers, keep a cardigan in your closet. When the mood hits, take a break, refresh, and have fun. You have earned it.

*****

One of the first questions you ask when you interview any person to work for a school system, in any capacity, is this: "What do you think of kids?"

If they don't tell you that they love kids, then don't hire them. No exceptions.

*****

Wisdom: Before you speak, listen. Before you write, think. Before you spend, earn. Before you invest, investigate. Before you criticize, wait. Before you pray, forgive. Before you quit, try. Before you retire, save. And, before you die, give.

William Arthur Ward

*****

Be a doorman (or doorlady). Meet the cars in the morning once in a while. Go up to the window and say "Hi" to the mom or dad and, of course, welcome the kid. If it's a high school, do it as well. You may want to wave from a distance if you think the driver might still be in their robe, curlers, or PJs! The important thing is to be visible, greet the kids, welcome the teachers, and wave at the parents. You don't have to do this every day, but when you do, you will find it pays dividends. It also helps to do this on rainy or snowy days when the drivers might need to be moved along to alleviate the heavier than normal traffic flow. And offering an umbrella helps too. A simple "thanks for bringing your child to school on a day like this!" goes a long way to brighten up a morning.

*****

Wise and Wherefores

Believe in miracles but don't depend on them.
When you hear a kind word spoken about a friend, tell him so.
Never order barbeque in a restaurant where all the chairs match.
Spoil your spouse, not your children.
Never make fun of people who speak broken English. It means they know another language.
Remember, it's not your job to get people to like you; it's you job to like people.
To help your children turn out well, spend twice as much time with them and half as much money.
Remember that the only dumb question is the one you wanted to ask but didn't.

H. Jackson Brown

*****

Want a clean school and clean grounds? Pick up the litter. That's right, you do it! When you see some, bend down and pick it up. Guess what, people will see you setting the example and they will do it too. If you are consistent with this behavior, and ask others to do the same, you will have a cleaner school, and build pride in the process.

*****

Here is a pledge for a school leader...

"I will not flinch in the face of sacrifice, hesitate in the presence of adversity, negotiate... at the table of the enemy, ponder at the pool of popularity, or meander in a maze of mediocrity. I won't give up, shut up, let up, or slow up."

Robert Moorehead

*****

When a teacher or a parent or a taxpayer in general tells you that you make too much money, don't defend your salary. Don't get angry. Don't engage in a discussion. Don't let them win. Ignore them, change the topic, or simply leave. If they don't understand how much you work and that you don't make as much as comparable jobs in other professions, you aren't going to change their minds. If they ask you to respond, tell them you don't set your own salary or your benefits and move on. Then don't fret about it. It will always be a point of discussion, as will be the fact that teachers get their summers off. Don't be rude, just don't get into it with them.

*****

My mother used to have her own grading schedule. An A was acceptable. A B meant you could do better. A C meant curfew. We think a D stood for death, and we never asked about the F. Maybe that is the reason why between all four of her kids there are 11 kinds of college degrees and at least 60 books written and published.

*****

The School Principal's Toolbook

Visit at least one teacher, in the classroom, every day. Even if it is only a 10-minute visit. Don't make your visits infrequent and out-of-the-ordinary. Let them know you are interested in how they teach. And say hello to as many every day as you can.

*****

The best things in life aren't things.

Ann Landers

*****

Don't be afraid to demonstrate your faith with your staff and your students. You can't teach it, or endorse it, but you can live it.

*****

Carry a clipboard during supervision time. On the clipboard have a list of students who are having some academic or behavior problems. You can ask teachers to give you this information or you can carry the most recent D/F list. When you see students on the list, quietly pull them aside and ask them how it is going. Ask what you can do to help. Maybe offer to arrange for a tutor. Ask them, or offer to help them, or do anything, but do it in a nonthreatening, nondisciplinary way. Let them know that you want to see them improve, that you are there to help, and to give them some encouragement. Be prepared to promptly follow up on anything you promise. This act, if done consistently, helps students improve. You will find that when students see that clipboard, some will voluntarily come up to you to report progress! It is amazing what will happens when they know you *really do care* and will act on it. Also, put notes of recognition, birthdays, awards, and other positive things on your clipboard so you can offer some congratulations when you see the student.

*****

Teaching kids to count is fine, but teaching them what counts is best.

Bob Talbert

*****

When I was named high school principal I really wanted to be back in the classroom. So I created an opportunity. I wrote a class that was offered on the days opposite driver's ed. Our students took driver's education every other day, and on the off days they went to study hall. My class was optional, and only yielded a partial credit. It was called LTS, which meant Love, Trust, and Success. It was a life skills class. We talked about everything: how to interview for a job, manners, different definitions of "love," how to cut off a relationship, respecting differences, and a long list of other things kids needed to know. It was great to teach and great to offer. After the first semester the enrollment was 100% of the eligible kids.

A recent issue of *Kappan Magazine* had an article by Richard Weissbourd, Amelia Peterson, and Emily Weinstein called "Preparing Students for Romantic Relationships." It reminded me of LTS, and it contained some great recommendations.

I recently had a message on Facebook from a former student. She said, "I learned a lot in high school, but what made the biggest difference in how I lived was what I learned in a class called Love, Trust, and Success." That post made my day.

*****

There are just two rules for success: (1) Never tell all you know.

Roger H. Lincoln

*****

The School Principal's Toolbook

I had a fifth-grade teacher who taught all his kids a unit on manners. They even had a "formal" meal one day with linens, china, and the whole enchilada. No, they didn't have enchiladas. They experienced the entire formal table setting and learned (and used) the manners that go with it. Kids loved it, but parents loved it even more. It was great and should have been a mandatory class.

*****

If you are patient in one moment of anger, you will escape a hundred days of sorrow.

Chinese proverb

*****

I was once hired by a superintendent in another state to be a "secret shopper" of his district. He asked me to visit, call, mail, do anything to test various aspects of how his district was perceived. He offered to cover my expenses and travel. I said it would be a pleasure and then asked him to do the same for my district. I visited his district, each school, and called each office. I went into each separate school office without an appointment to "gather information" for a possible move to the community, bringing my family. My pretend family included a primary level student, an upper elementary special needs student, a high school freshman, and a student that would need residential care. I was talking about an expensive family for any school district to accept. I met each building secretary, met two principals, took three tours and even met with a real estate agent to see if they recommended the school district. I also had a haircut downtown to get input from the barber and customers. I gave a written report to the superintendent. It included my impression of the grounds, signage, attitude of the staff, comments from the community, and an overall first impression of a newbie coming to town. I ranked the employees I met and shared many positive comments, as well as disappointments. I was totally honest. I included the quality of their website as well.

The School Principal's Toolbook

My report helped him make many improvements during his tenure there, and even resulted in the removal of one staff member, after an appropriate investigation. I recommend this process to principals and superintendents alike. It helps. His review of my district was equally as informative and helpful.

*****

Send the members of the board of education an unexpected thank-you card. Let them know you appreciate what they do. Will your nose turn brown? Not if the note comes from your heart. I wonder how many board members receive thank-you notes after agreeing to an increase in wages, or for being willing to give their time for no pay, or for attending concerts or ball games when they don't have a student involved? Send a copy to the superintendent as well with a thank you to him or her.

*****

Two hunters chartered a plane to fly them into a remote region in Canada so that they might hunt for elk. When the plane returned for them a few days later, their hunt had been successful. The two hunters had six elk to show for their effort.

When the pilot explained to them that his plane could only carry four of the elk, the hunters protested, "But the plane that we chartered last year was exactly like this one. It had the same horsepower, the weather was similar, and we took out six elk then."

Hearing this, the pilot reluctantly agreed to load all six elk. The plane struggled during takeoff, and was unable to gain sufficient altitude to climb out of the valley. It crashed near the top of a mountain. To their great fortune, all three men survived.

As the hunters stumbled out of the wreckage, one of them asked the dazed pilot, "Do you know where we are?" He mumbled, "No." The other hunter, however, looked around and said confidently, "I think we're about a mile from where we crashed last year!"

The School Principal's Toolbook

Mistakes are meant to lead to wisdom, not to future error. Just as children should draw lessons from skinned knees and bruised elbows, adults need to convert mistakes into lessons for improvement.

*****

If you see students doing something neat, like helping another student that fell, or picking up litter without being asked, stop by their classroom with a soda (or some politically correct item) *one for each student*—and tell them why you are there and who is responsible. The reaction will amaze you. Do the same for teachers, giving every student an apple because their teacher did something cool. Doing this will in itself be cool.

*****

People who live well are experts at giving. They give their money; they give their time. They share their wisdom and their skills. They quickly say yes when asked to help. For them... to give is to love and to love is to live. It's a formula for a successful life.

Steve Goodier

*****

Ask your secretary, or peers, to keep you informed about who is getting married, who had a baby, who died, who is sick, and all the "people" information *that everyone will assume you know so they don't tell you.* This is very important. Then respond with cards, flowers, notes, gifts, whatever is appropriate.

******

Return phone calls ASAP, if not sooner! If you are out of the office, tell your secretary or staff to inform your callers, or visitors, when you are expected to return. People like honest communications. If you are in and can't take the call, have your secretary say so. It doesn't help to hear something like, "I'll see

The School Principal's Toolbook

if he/she is in," or "Who may I say is calling?" followed by, "He/she can't talk right now." It is a lot easier to hear something like, "I know he/she is in, but they may have someone in their office. Let me check for you." Never have your secretary tell the caller *when* you will return the call. That may set up a negative situation if you don't call back during that time frame. You need to coordinate phone message procedures carefully with your secretary or the receptionist.

Finally, have your assistant communicate honesty. Never say you aren't there if you are. Have them say you can't come to the phone right now but will look forward to calling back as soon as possible. Then do it.

Incidentally, I recently called a school to talk to the principal. The responder said, "She's gone again and we don't know where or when she will be back, as usual!" You don't want this to happen to you!

*****

One person with passion is better than forty who are merely interested.

Tom Connellan

*****

Never have your secretary make calls for you and then have the party wait while she gets you on the phone. *No one* appreciates this. *No one.*

*****

Be careful of anger—it's just one letter away from danger.

Ivan Donthvaclu

*****

If it is crazy hat day, wear a crazy hat. It they are painting paw prints on everyone's cheek at the championship ball game, have one painted on your cheek. Stand up and cheer when the cheerleaders ask the fans to do so—in fact, be the first one.

*****

Make a habit to tell people, "thank you." Express your appreciation, sincerely and without any expectation, of anything in return. Truly appreciate those around you, and you'll soon find many others around you. Truly appreciate life, and you'll find that you may have more of it.

Ralph Marsten

*****

Send thank-you notes to anyone who takes the time to write you a recommendation, or helps you in any way. To not send a thank you is simply rude.

*****

Cry at funerals. Laugh at jokes. Hug babies. Look at and compliment wedding pictures. Be real. Enjoy life. Don't always be the boss. Take time to be a human too. When teachers come back from having a baby, stop to visit them asking to see pictures. And remember, if you are too busy to listen to or talk to an employee, then you are simply too busy.

*****

If you don't go after what you want, you'll never have it. If you don't ask, the answer is always no. If you don't step forward, you're always in the same place.

Norah Jones

*****

Keep a handful of nice greeting cards in your desk (not the ones you get free from some organization that wants a donation). Use them for the birthday, illness, or other situations that might require a personal note. Emailing and texting are nice, but on the thoughtful scale they don't compare with an old-fashioned, time-required, you-forked-out money-for-it greeting card.

*****

When there are new learning standards to study, when you are faced with PERRA or PARCC, or some national mandate or new state assessment program, or a new licensure requirement, dig into it, be positive about it, step forward and embrace the requirement, making its importance your importance. If there are problems with it, if it is not realistic, or if you can't fulfill it with current staff or resources, share those issues while doing what you can to be a good soldier. The administrator who cooperates and leads positively, while also trying to improve programs purposefully and respectfully, will always shine and have the greatest results. Be that administrator.

*****

Is all you do worth it? Think about the message in this old Chinese proverb:

One generation plants the trees under whose shade another generation rests.

*****

When you take a call from someone and they put you on hold, never wait more than two minutes. Hang up. They will call you back or you can call them back later. Your time is worth something too. If you have a speakerphone, use it when you are on hold so you can continue to do work while you are waiting. If you use a speakerphone when you are talking, ask if the connection is clear first, and if using the speakerphone is acceptable. You want your listener to think that the call is your priority. Try not to do other (obvious) work while talking (like typing, talking to others, opening and closing file cabinets, etc.). It's just called *common courtesy.*

The School Principal's Toolbook

*****

The longer I live, the more I realize the impact of attitude on life. Attitude to me is more important than facts. It is more important than the past, than education, than money, than circumstance, than failures, than success, than what other people think, say or do. It is more important than appearance, gift, or skill. It will make or break a company, a church, or a home. The remarkable thing is we have a choice every day regarding the attitude we will embrace for that day. We cannot change our past... The only thing we can do is play on the string we have, and that is our attitude... I am convinced that life is 10 percent what happens to me and 90 percent how I react to it. And so it is with you... We are in charge of our attitudes.

Charles Swindoll

*****

What does this say? **OPPORTUNITYISNOWHERE**

Did you read it as...

Opportunity is *nowhere*
      or
Opportunity is *now, here*?

******

Carry a rubber hammer, a set of chattering teeth, a "laughing bag," or any other toy that causes someone to laugh. Use them appropriately and when needed. Make an announcement to school in the middle of the normal announcements that doesn't make sense, like, "I was just told that due to the weather school will be canceled tomorrow (when tomorrow is Saturday)." Just have fun and be unpredictable. It pays huge dividends.

*****

The School Principal's Toolbook

251

Each day is God's gift to you. What you do with it is your gift to Him.

T. D. Jakes

*****

When kids cry, hug them. When teachers hurt, console them. When your family needs you, be with them. Know your priorities and don't let anything keep you from them.

*****

I see children as kites. You spend a lifetime trying to get them off the ground. You run with them until you're both breathless... they crash... they hit the rooftop... you patch and comfort, adjust and teach. You watch them lifted by the wind and assure them that someday they'll fly. Finally they are airborne: they need more string and you keep letting it out. But with each twist of the ball of twine, there is a sadness that goes with joy. The kite becomes more distant, and you know it won't be long before that beautiful creature will snap the lifeline that binds you together and will soar as it is meant to soar, free and alone. Only then do you know that you did your job.

Erma Bombeck

*****

Never lie. Not to anyone. Not even to the IRS. No matter how you cut it, a lie is a lie.

*****

Luck is a dividend of sweat. The more you sweat the luckier you get.

Ray Kroc

*****

A school leader has inherited the obligation of being a role model. Look in the mirror and ask yourself, if you were a child, would you want to grow up like you?

*****

Instead of putting others in their place, try putting yourself in their place.

Unknown

*****

Recipe for greatness: To bear up under loss; to fight the bitterness of defeat and the weakness of grief: to be a victor over anger; to smile when tears are close; to resist evil men and base instincts; to hate hate and love love; to go on when it would seem good to die; to seek ever after the glory and the dream; to look up with unquenchable faith in something ever more about to be; that is what any man can do and so be great.

Zane Grey

*****

And finally, a good friend of mine, Dr. John Butts, reminds us all...

On our worst day, we have it better than most places do on their best day.

"Nothing lowers the level of conversation more than raising the voice."

Stanley Horowitz, poet/civil leader

Epilogue

The School Principal's Toolbook: Building the How-To Path to Excellence is a book about sharing. It is what we do in this profession—we share. There is little competition among school leaders. If we discover something that works, instead of hoarding it to build our own kingdom, we are eager to share it with others. Our collective kingdom is the education of kids. There seems to be a desire to continually dig for new ways, new ideas, and new concepts. And when we strike gold we want to put it on a blog, write an article, hold a seminar—share the wealth. That is exactly what this toolbook is designed to do.

As the author I can only say that most of what was assembled in these pages reflects the passion and intelligence of those who have and are working to improve educational opportunities for children everywhere. It is a collaboration of their efforts.

As a building administrator told me this very day, "Once you get school administration in your blood, it is hard to find anything so rewarding, so perplexing, and so challenging."

When you watch a school become an exceptional place to learn, when you witness a teacher blossom into one of those special people who will become unforgettable for all the right reasons, and when you can feel in your heart that you have helped dent the universe, then you realize the honor of being the leader, the principal, and the difference maker.

Thanks for what you do. I hope this book will help you do it even better.

Bibliography

Blanchard, Ken, and Johnson, S., *The One Minute Manager*. New York: William Morrow, 1982.

Bowles, S., Silvano, R., and Silvano S., *Kingdomality*. New York: Hyperion, 2005.

Burgett, J., *The Art of School Boarding: What Every Board Member Must Know*. Novato, CA: Education Communication Unlimited, 2013.

------, *Teachers Change Lives 24/7*. Novato, CA: Education Communication Unlimited, 2008.

------, and Schwartz, B., *Finding Middle Ground in K-12 Education: Balancing Best Practices and the Law*. Novato, CA: Education Communication Unlimited, 2009.

Collins, J., *God to Great*. New York: Harper Collins, 2001.

------, *Great by Choice*. New York: Harper Collins, 2011.

Cottrell, D., *Leadership Secrets of Santa Claus*. Dallas: Walk the Talk, 2003.

Fullan, M., *The Principal*. San Francisco: Jossey-Bass, 2014.

Harvey, E., and Cottrell, D., Lucia, A., and Houngan, M., *Leadership Courage*. Dallas: Walk the Talk, 2004.

Isaacson, W., *Steve Jobs*. New York: Simon and Schuster, 2011.

Jones, L., *Jesus CEO*. New York: Hyperion, 1992.

Mandino, O., *The Greatest Salesman in the World*. New York: Bantam, 1983.

Marzano, R., Waters, T., and McNulty, B., *School Leadership That Works*. Aurora, CO: Mid-Continent Research, 2005.

Maxwell, J., *Everyone Communicates, Few Connect*. Nashville: Thomas Nelson, 2010.

------, *Failing Forward*. Nashville: Thomas Nelson, 2000.

------, *Sometimes You Win, Sometimes You Learn*. New York: Center Street, 2013.

------, *The 17 Essential Qualities of a Team Player*. Nashville: Thomas Nelson, 2002.

------, *The 21 Indispensable Qualities of a Leader*. Nashville: Thomas Nelson, 1999.

Murphy, J., *Pulling Together*. Naperville, IL: Simple Truths, 2009.

Myatt, M., *Hacking Leadership*, Hoboken, NJ: Wiley, 2014.

Phillips, D., *Lincoln on Leadership*. New York: Warner Books, 1993.

Rosborg, J., McGee, M., and Burgett, J., *What Every Superintendent and Principal Needs to Know*. Novato, CA: Education Communication Unlimited, 2006.

-----, McGee, M., and Burgett, J., *The Perfect School*. Novato, CA: Education Communication Unlimited, 2007.

Strunk, W., and White, E.B., *The Elements of Style*. New York: Longman, 1959.

Whitaker, T., *What Great Principals Do Differently*. New York: Eye on Education, 2012.

Williamson, R., and Johnson, H., *The School Leader's Guide to Social Media*. New York: Eye on Education, 2012.

Wooden, J., and Jamison, S., *My Personal Best*. New York: McGraw Hill, 2004.

Index

More Books for K-12 Administrators and Teachers

Education Communication Unlimited

The Art of
School Boarding:
What Every School Board
Member Needs to Know

Jim Burgett

The Kid in Purple Pants

Pat Anderson

For more book and ordering
information see
meetingK-12needs.com

Finding Middle Ground
in K-12 Education

Jim Burgett / Brian Schwartz

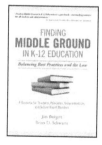

The Perfect School

Jim Rosborg / Max McGee /
Jim Burgett

For more book and ordering
information see
meetingK-12needs.com

Teachers Change Lives 24/7

Jim Burgett